The Book of
Weird
Mysteries

John Hawkins

This edition published in 2025 by Arcturus Publishing Limited
26/27 Bickels Yard, 151–153 Bermondsey Street,
London SE1 3HA

Copyright © Arcturus Holdings Limited

All rights reserved. No part of this publication may be reproduced, stored in a retrieval system, or transmitted, in any form or by any means, electronic, mechanical, photocopying, recording, or otherwise, without prior written permission in accordance with the provisions of the Copyright Act 1956 (as amended). Any person or persons who do any unauthorized act in relation to this publication may be liable to criminal prosecution and civil claims for damages.

Picture Credits:
Art Archive/Kobal: 4tr, 36. B. Barber: 17. Bill Stoneham: 74. Corbis: 1tc, 2tr, 2b, 4tl, 4tc, 4bl, 10, 12, 14, 16, 17, 19, 21, 22, 23, 24, 28, 32, 34, 35, 39, 40, 41, 43, 44, 46, 47, 53, 54, 55, 56, 62, 64, 68, 81, 93, 100, 102, 113, 123, 124. Cryptomundo.com: 85. Frank Joseph: 1tr, 60, 61, 67, 69, 71, 72, 73. Getty: 27, 50. Idaho State University: 86. iStockphoto: 4c, 105, 109, 110, 116, 117. Mary Evans Picture Library: 7, 8, 9, 11, 13, 18, 42, 45, 48, 49, 52, 92. P. Gray: 20. Science Photo Library: 33. Shutterstock: 1tl, 1br, 2t, 2c, 2cr, 4bc, 25, 26, 29, 37, 51, 57, 58, 59, 63, 66, 70, 77, 78, 79, 80, 83, 84, 94, 95, 96, 98, 103, 104, 106, 107, 108, 111, 115, 119. T. Boyer: 30, 31. TopFoto: 1bl, 38, 76, 87, 89, 90. Wikimedia: 1bc, 88, 97. William Stoneham: 82, 91.

Author: John Hawkins
Designer and Editor: Lucy Doncaster
US Editor: Kara Murray
Editorial Manager: Joe Harris
Design Manager: Rosie Bellwood

ISBN: 978-1-3988-5046-0
CH012437NT
Supplier 13, Date 0425, PI 00009335

Printed in China

CONTENTS

Introduction 4

ALIENS 6
The UFOs Arrive 6
The "First" UFO 8
The Roswell Incident 10
The Mantell Incident 12
The Botta Encounter 14
The Kelly-Hopkinsville Encounter 16
The Interrupted Journey 18
The Socorro Incident 20
Incident at Valensole 22
The Exeter Incident 24
Man in Black 26
Fatal Encounter at Bass Strait 28
The Livingston UFO Assault 30

HAUNTINGS 32
Ancient Apparitions 32
Fateful Appearances 34
Ghosts of War 36
Living Apparitions 38
Talking to the Dead 40
Possession 42
The Bloody Tower 44
The Ghosts of Glamis 46
Noises in the Night 48
Tombstone 50
Borley Rectory 52
Alcatraz 54

LOST LANDS 56
What Was Atlantis? 56
What Was Lemuria? 58
Seekers of Atlantis 60
Technology of Atlantis 62
How Were Atlantis and Lemuria Destroyed? 64
Legacy of Atlantis: North Africa and Europe 66
Legacy of Atlantis: The Americas 68
The Search for Atlantis: The Northeast Atlantic 70
The Search for Atlantis: The Caribbean 72
The Search for Lemuria 74
Lost Worlds of the Americas 76
Lost Worlds of the North 78
Shambhala 80

MONSTERS 82
Bigfoot: First Impressions 82
Bigfoot: The Sightings Continue 84
Bigfoot: Hitting the Headlines 86
Bigfoot: Filming a Sasquatch 88
The Skunk Ape 90
The Yeti 92
The Big Gray Man 94
The Loch Ness Monster 96
Nessie: The Hunt Continues 98
The Lusca 100
The Mongolian Death Worm 102
Mothman 104
The Ogopogo 106

MYSTERIES 108
Crop Circles 108
The Bermuda Triangle 110
The Nazca Lines 112
The Piri Reis Map 114
King Arthur 116
Ghost Ship 118
The Secret Princess 120
The Immortal Count 122
An Uncanny Child 124

Index 126

▲ Clockwise, from top left: The Lusca; a movie prop of an alien; protective angels in World War I; the Great Pyramid in Giza, Egypt; the architecture of Atlantis; the Sword in the Stone.

INTRODUCTION

We live in a world of possibility, where the fantastical can become fact and the miraculous can become mundane. If you were to travel back just a hundred years and tell your recent relatives that one day humans would be able to send a mission to Mars, bounce signals off satellites in space to order groceries, or even to fight infection with a simple pill, they would be hard-pressed to believe you. And yet all of these things are true.

In light of this, is it such a stretch to accept that other seemingly incredible or mysterious events could also have happened? After all, tales of ghosts, aliens, strange creatures, and lost lands have been told and handed down from generation to generation by countless people all over the planet, often for hundreds or even thousands of years. For example, the afterlife and the spectral beings who inhabit the domain of the dead have been a topic of conversation since the time of the ancient Egyptians, and possibly even earlier!

So, it makes sense that we too should open our minds to contemplate more fully the weird and wonderful world around us. This book will guide you through some of the most intriguing cases and tell the stories of those who have witnessed all manner of strange goings-on. From aliens and apparitions to monsters, lost lands, and other unexplained phenomena, get ready to take a leap of faith and explore the riveting realm of the great unknown.

THE UFOS ARRIVE

Public interest in UFOs, or unidentified flying objects, really began with the startling encounter reported by American pilot Kenneth Arnold in 1947. However, mysterious flying objects had been seen in the skies for many years before then. For example, cigar-shaped craft were seen over the United States in the 1890s, although these were probably early airships.

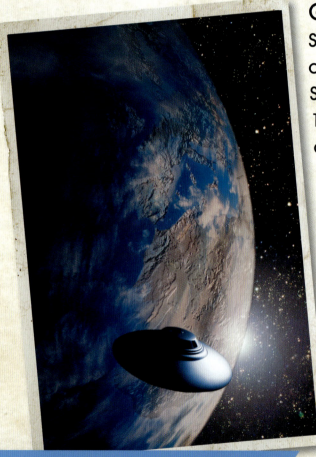

▲ Many UFOlogists believe that Earth has regularly been visited by aliens since the 1940s.

GHOST FLIERS

So-called ghost fliers were spotted on a number of occasions over Scandinavia between 1932 and 1937. In daylight, they took the form of very large aircraft—much bigger than anything then flying.

At night, they shone dazzlingly bright searchlights onto the ground. According to eyewitness reports, they performed aerobatics and achieved speeds utterly impossible for any known aircraft.

FOO FIGHTERS

During World War II, strange glowing balls about 1 m (3 ft) across, known as foo fighters, were seen over Europe by pilots from both sides of the war.

▼ An illustration of a pair of foo fighters flying alongside a USAF B-24 Liberator bomber in 1944.

They were observed flying alongside bomber formations for minutes at a time before either disappearing or flying off at high speed.

Pilots on both sides of the conflict assumed they were some form of enemy weapon and tried to shoot them down. But bullets appeared to have no effect on the crafts. What they actually were has never been discovered.

Examining The Evidence

Are UFOs real?

The witnesses whose stories have been told in this book were probably telling the truth, and believed they really did experience a visitation from another planet. But could their senses have been deceiving them? They might have misidentified astronomical objects such as clouds, planets, bright stars, meteors, artificial satellites, or the Moon. A number of UFO reports have been explained by flights of secret aircraft, weapons, and weather balloons or by light phenomena such as mirages and searchlights. Other UFO stories have turned out to be deliberate hoaxes. However, some UFO sightings have never been fully explained.

THE "FIRST" UFO

On the morning of June 24, 1947, Kenneth Arnold, an experienced American aviator, set off from Chehalis, Washington, to his home in Oregon in his single-engine Callier light aircraft. While flying over Mount Rainier, Arnold saw something that would change his life and usher in a new era.

FLASH OF LIGHT

Arnold saw a bright flash of light sweep over his plane. Assuming this was caused by the sunlight reflecting off another nearby aircraft, Arnold hurriedly scanned the skies. Far to the north he saw a line of nine aircraft flying toward him at an angle.

▲ This artwork, signed by Kenneth Arnold, shows the aircraft he claimed to have seen. Arnold himself appears bottom left.

As they came closer, Arnold realized that he was seeing something very strange indeed. Each aircraft was shaped like a wide crescent and had neither fuselage nor tail. What's more, the aircraft were flying with a strange wavelike motion, quite unlike that of any known aircraft. They dipped from side to side at times, the sunlight reflecting from their silver-blue surfaces.

The formation was moving very fast. Arnold later estimated the speed at around 2,100 km/h (1,300 mph)—much faster than any known aircraft at that time.

FLYING SAUCERS

When he reached home, Arnold contacted a reporter, Bill Bacquette, at the *East Oregonian*, his local newspaper. Bacquette asked how the craft moved. Arnold said, "They flew like a saucer would if you skipped it across water." In his report, Bacquette referred to the craft as flying saucers. The term quickly became popular.

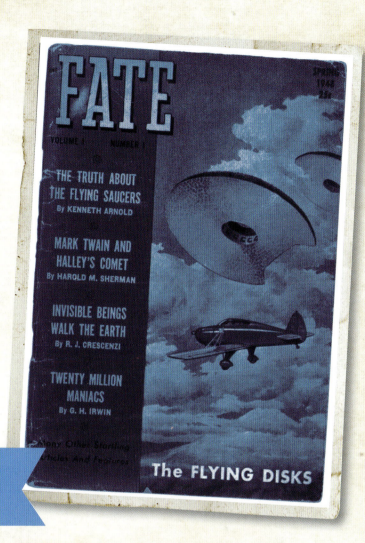

▶ *Fate* magazine, launched in 1948, led its first edition with the Arnold sighting.

STRANGE STORIES

TWO SHADOWS

Arnold's experience prompted others to come forward with their own stories. A group of boys from Baradine, Australia, were rabbiting by moonlight one night in 1931. One boy noticed he was casting two shadows. Looking up, he saw a disc-shaped object as bright as the Moon approaching from the northwest. Orange lights or flames flashed around its rim and the object rotated slowly as it flew. It followed a straight course before disappearing behind nearby hills.

THE ROSWELL INCIDENT

What really happened in early July 1947 at Roswell Air Force Base? On July 8, a press release from the base stated that a flying saucer had crashed near Roswell and the wreckage had been recovered. A few hours later, a second press release stated that the wreckage was actually from a weather balloon.

THE STORY IS REVIVED

Thirty years later, UFO researcher Stanton Friedman was put in touch with a former intelligence officer, Jesse Marcel, who served at Roswell. Marcel claimed he had been sent to the crash site to collect the debris and had never believed the weather balloon story. Friedman and his colleague William Moore also tracked down other witnesses.

▼ This movie prop depicting an alien crash victim is on display at the International UFO Museum and Research Center, in Roswell.

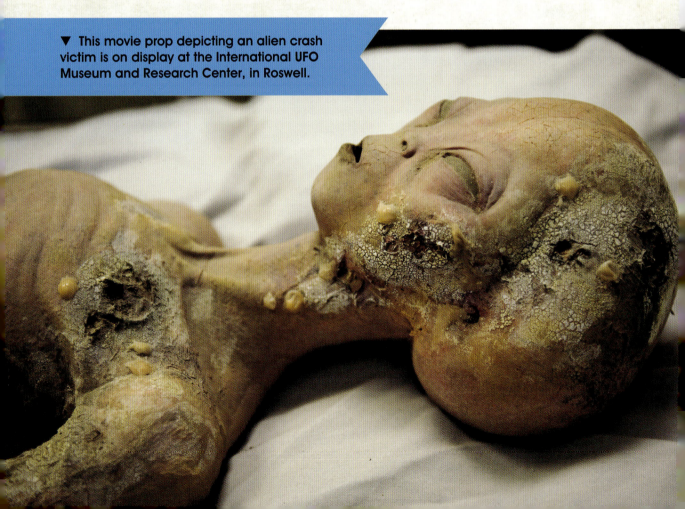

▲ In response to press interest in the Roswell incident, in 1947, the US military released this image showing the wreckage from a weather balloon. But was this part of a cover-up?

ALIEN BODIES?

In 1989, a mortician (a person who prepares dead bodies for burial) named Glenn Dennis claimed that the USAF medical team had called him in July 1947. He said they asked him detailed questions about how to preserve bodies. A USAF photographer then said he had seen and photographed four alien bodies at the base.

WITNESS INTERVIEWS

By 1980, Friedman and Moore had interviewed 62 people. They believed something strange had happened at Roswell and that the United States Air Force (USAF) had covered it up. The witnesses claimed to have seen a UFO performing moves impossible for any known aircraft. A rancher, W. "Mac" Brazel, had heard an explosion and found mysterious debris.

Examining The Evidence

A different kind of cover-up?

Most of the evidence at Roswell was collected decades after the event, and not all of it was firsthand. An official USAF report has dismissed Friedman's claims. It admitted there had been a cover-up, but this was because the crashed craft had been a top-secret Mogul high-altitude balloon, used for spying on the Soviets. However, many UFOlogists remain convinced that the USAF covered up something much more mysterious at Roswell.

THE MANTELL INCIDENT

At lunchtime on January 7, 1948, a UFO was spotted over Godman Air Force Base, in Kentucky. Colonel Guy Hix, commander at Godman, scrambled three P-51 fighter aircraft, which set off in pursuit of the mysterious object.

GIVING CHASE

Flight Commander Captain Thomas Mantell saw the object first as the three aircraft emerged from the clouds. The other two pilots radioed to say that they could see the object and Mantell's aircraft giving chase. But then clouds closed in again and the two pilots lost sight of both the object and Mantell.

Shortly afterward, they returned to base. Mantell, meanwhile, was in hot pursuit. He sent three radio messages with updates on his progress, then nothing. After several minutes of radio silence from Mantell, Hix began to worry. More aircraft were scrambled to search the skies for the mysterious object and for Mantell's P-51, but they saw nothing.

▲ Three fighter jets were scrambled to intercept the UFO over Kentucky.

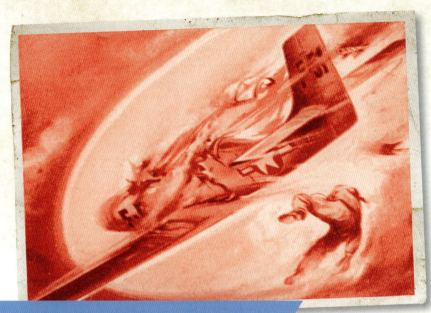

▲ This artist's impression captures the moment that Captain Mantell's P-51 Mustang fighter broke up in the air.

FATAL CRASH

A few hours later, the wreckage of Mantell's aircraft was found strewn over a large area of countryside. It had obviously broken up at high altitude and fallen to the ground in thousands of pieces. The P-51 was a famously robust fighter jet that did not fall to pieces for no reason.

The death of Mantell turned the UFO phenomenon into an issue of deadly seriousness. It seemed unlikely that the USAF would allow its pilots to chase after one of their own secret weapons, and equally unlikely that the Soviet Union would risk testing secret aircraft in US airspace. So what did Mantell and his fellow pilots chase that day? We still have no idea.

EYEWITNESS TO MYSTERY

MANTELL'S FINAL RADIO MESSAGES

"The object is directly ahead of and above me now, moving at about half my speed … It looks metallic and it's tremendous in size."
A few minutes later: "I'm still climbing … I'm trying to close in for a better look."
Last message: "It is still above me, making my speed or better. I'm going up to 20,000 feet [6,000 m]. If I'm no closer then, I'll abandon the chase."

THE BOTTA ENCOUNTER

Dr. Enrique Botta was an engineer working on a building project in the rural area of Bahía Blanca in Venezuela. One evening in 1950, he was driving back to his hotel when he saw a strange object resting in a field. He stopped the car to take a look.

▼ Those who claim to have encountered aliens most often describe them as having bald, domed heads and large, black eyes.

INVESTIGATING THE OBJECT

According to Botta, the object was shaped like a domed disc made of a silvery metal. Its skin had a jellylike softness. There was an open door on one side. Botta walked through the door. He passed through a small, empty room into a second, larger room.

Here he saw three humanoid figures facing away from him. Each figure was about 1.2 m (4 ft) tall. Their heads were large and bald. They were facing a control panel filled with lights. Botta reached out and touched one of the figures. It was rigid. Believing the beings were dead, Botta fled back to his car.

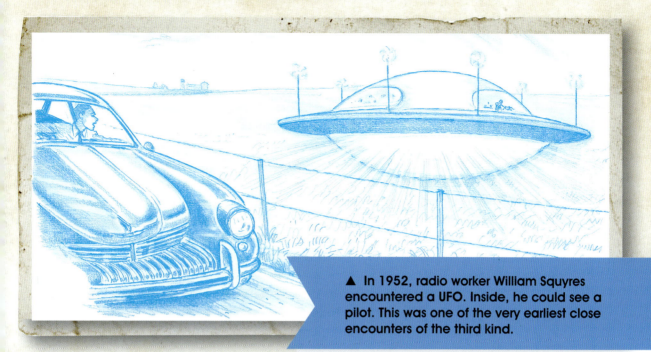

▲ In 1952, radio worker William Squyres encountered a UFO. Inside, he could see a pilot. This was one of the very earliest close encounters of the third kind.

RETURN TO THE SITE

Botta told two of his colleagues at the hotel, and the three returned to the site the next morning. The craft had gone and all that remained was a pile of ashes. One of Botta's friends touched the pile and his hand turned purple. Botta, meanwhile, spotted a cigar-shaped UFO circling overhead. After a few minutes it flew away. Later that day, Botta collapsed with a fever and was rushed to hospital where he was diagnosed with severe sunburn.

FACT HUNTER

CLOSE ENCOUNTERS

- **WHAT ARE THEY?**

Encounters with UFOs have been divided into three kinds:

- Close encounters of the first kind (CE1s) —sightings of UFOs

- Close encounters of the second kind (CE2s)—observation of UFOs and their physical effects, such as crop circles

- Close encounters of the third kind (CE3s) —observation of aliens

When was the first CE3? The first reported CE3 took place in 1952 when radio worker William Squyres spotted a humanoid at the controls of a disc-shaped UFO hovering above a field in Kansas.

THE KELLY-HOPKINSVILLE ENCOUNTER

On August 21, 1955, Bill Taylor was visiting the Sutton family at their remote farm between Kelly and Hopkinsville, Kentucky. At around 7 p.m., Taylor was getting water from the well when, he says, he saw a disc-shaped UFO floating down behind a line of trees.

STRANGE VISITOR

An hour later, Taylor and Elmer Sutton were in the kitchen when they saw a strange figure outside. They later claimed that it was around 1 m (3 ft) tall, walking upright on short legs, and with very long, apelike arms. The creature had a large head, pointed ears, bulging eyes, and a slitlike mouth. It emitted a soft, silvery glow.

The being was joined by several more, which began wandering around the farmyard. Sutton and Taylor picked up their guns and stepped out of the house. Sutton shouted a challenge. What did these beings want?

One of the aliens ran at them with its arms above its head. Sutton

▲ According to Bill Taylor, the aliens that attacked the Sutton family emerged from a UFO he had seen landing nearby.

UNDER SIEGE

Taylor and Sutton returned to the house and heard footsteps on the roof. As Taylor stepped out, one of the aliens grabbed his hair. Whipping around, he shot the alien. It flipped backward over the roof, then fled into the darkness.

For the next three hours, the family remained inside the house while the men took potshots at the aliens whenever they appeared. In the morning, they drove to the Hopkinsville police station and reported their story. The police found evidence of a battle at the farm but no aliens.

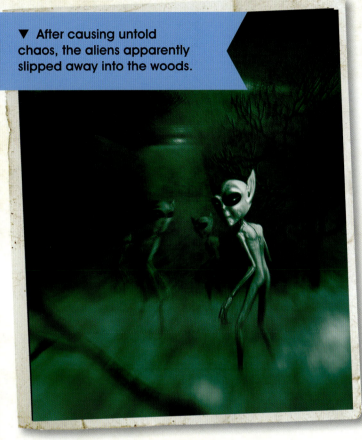

▼ After causing untold chaos, the aliens apparently slipped away into the woods.

fired. The impact knocked the being onto its back. After a moment, it got back to its feet and ran off, uninjured.

EYEWITNESS TO MYSTERY

"SOMETHING FRIGHTENED THESE PEOPLE"

Elmer Sutton was known in the area as a cool, tough farmer, not given to flights of fancy. The Suttons' story seemed outlandish, but the local police were inclined to take it seriously. Chief of Police Russell Greenwell later commented: "Something frightened these people. Something beyond their comprehension." Despite suffering ridicule, the Suttons and Taylor never changed their story. They remained convinced that they had come under attack that night and had been lucky to escape with their lives.

THE INTERRUPTED JOURNEY

At about 11 p.m. on September 19, 1961, Betty and Barney Hill were driving along Highway 3 near Lancaster, New Hampshire, when they saw a bright light in the sky. They pulled over to watch the object.

TIME DISCREPANCY

The object was oval-shaped and bluish-white. Through the row of windows on its front edge, humanoids could be seen moving around. Barney suddenly panicked. Convinced they were about to be attacked, he ushered his wife back into the car and then took off at high speed. They returned home at 5 a.m. and went straight to bed.

Five days later, Betty contacted UFOlogist Donald Keyhoe. Keyhoe pointed out that the encounter had lasted only a few minutes, yet they were two hours late getting home.

▲ According to Betty and Barney Hill, they could remember being followed in their car by a UFO but not what happened next.

In the months following the encounter, Betty and Barney suffered from disturbing nightmares and depression. When their regular doctor couldn't help, they were sent to see Dr. Benjamin Simon, who specialized in hypnotic regression.

▲ If aliens really do live among us, what are their plans for planet Earth?

TAKEN ABOARD

While under hypnosis, the Hills both said that their car was stopped by aliens standing in the road and that they were then taken to a landed UFO. Betty was forced to undergo painful medical experiments, then an alien showed her a map of the location of its home star system. The couple were eventually taken back to their car, after being told that they would not remember anything about the event.

FACT HUNTER

ALIEN ABDUCTIONS

- **WHAT ARE THEY?**
Alien abductions are seemingly real memories people have of being taken against their will by nonhuman entities and subjected to physical and psychological tests.

- **WHEN DID THEY START HAPPENING?**
The first case to gain widespread attention was that of Antonio Villas Boas, a Brazilian farmer, who claimed to have been abducted by aliens in 1957.

- **HAVE THERE BEEN MANY CASES?**
There have been many hundreds of cases, particularly in the United States.

- **DO THEY REALLY HAPPEN?**
Most scientists believe that alien abductions do not really happen but are a product of fantasy, false-memory syndrome, hallucination, hypnosis, and other psychological phenomena.

THE SOCORRO INCIDENT

On April 24, 1964, at around 5.45 p.m., Patrolman Lonnie Zamora was heading south from Socorro, New Mexico, in his police car in pursuit of a speeding motorist. He suddenly noticed a flash of bluish-orange in the sky to the west, followed by a roaring explosion. Fearing that the nearby dynamite shack had exploded, he gave up his chase to investigate.

▲ This artwork is based on Zamora's description of the craft and aliens.

TWO FIGURES

Zamora turned onto a rough gravel track. As he dipped into a shallow gully, the flame came again. It was shaped like a cone with the top narrower than the bottom. As he reached the top of the gully, Zamora saw an object with two figures standing beside it. The figures were wearing white overalls and may have had rounded caps or helmets on their heads.

THE OBJECT

When he looked again, the figures had vanished. Zamora got out of the car and approached the

▲ UFO believers cite Patrolman Lonnie Zamora as a reliable witness because of his position of responsibility.

see the object hovering on its flame above the ground. Next time he looked, the flame and the roaring had stopped and the object hung eerily motionless in the air. It then moved silently off toward the southwest before vanishing behind some hills.

object, which was whitish-silver and shaped like an oval standing on four legs. When Zamora was around 23 m (75 ft) from the object, a roaring began and a bluish-orange flame erupted from the base of the craft.

Fearing for his life, Zamora turned and ran. He glanced back from a safer distance to

Examining The Evidence

Analyzing the traces

A prominent UFOlogist, Dr. Josef Allen Hynek, was at the site two days later. He found burn marks on the ground where the craft had stood. Four deep rectangular marks were seen in the ground where heavy objects had pushed down into the dry soil. The marks were arranged as if on the circumference of a circle, as they would have been if there were four legs supporting a round object. Zamora was an excellent witness who was highly respected by his colleagues. Hynek concluded that a real, physical event of an unexplained nature had taken place.

ALIENS 21

INCIDENT AT VALENSOLE

Maurice Masse was a farmer in Valensole, France, one of the most rural parts of western Europe. He had no interest in UFOs and had never seen or read a science fiction movie or book. He had no obvious reason to invent a story. Yet here is what he claimed happened to him one July morning in 1965.

WHISTLING SOUND

Masse had stopped his tractor for a break when he heard a whistling sound coming from the other side of a small hill. He walked around the hill to investigate. He saw an egg-shaped, silver object mounted on six thin metal legs. Next to it were what he took to be two young boys with their backs to him, pulling at a lavender plant. Thinking they were vandals, he crept toward them.

PARALYZED

One of the "boys" turned around and whipped out a small gun-shaped object, which he pointed at Masse. The farmer suddenly

▲ Masse's description of the "aliens" he encountered is remarkably consistent with the accounts of other witnesses.

realized he was paralyzed. He could only look at the figures. They were about 1.2 m (4 ft) tall and had thin, slender bodies. Their heads were oval with pointy chins and large, slanting eyes. Their mouths were thin, lipless slits.

DEPARTURE

The figures made strange noises, but their mouths did not move. They floated up through an open hatch in the side of their craft, which rose vertically to around 18 m (60 ft), then flew away.

STRANGE STORIES

SIMILARITIES WITH SOCORRO

Some years after the incident at Valensole, a French UFO investigator sent Masse a drawing of the UFO that had landed at Socorro, New Mexico (see pages 20–21), as he thought it sounded similar. Masse's reaction was immediate and emphatic: "That is what I saw," he replied. "You see: I was not dreaming and I was not mad."

▲ This artist's impression of alien creatures is based on Maurice Masse's description.

THE EXETER INCIDENT

At 1 a.m. on September 3, 1965, Patrolman Eugene Bertrand was driving along Route 108 near Exeter, New Hampshire, when he saw a car parked by the side of the road. He pulled over and found a woman in some distress. She said her car had been followed by a bright white light in the sky, which had hovered over the vehicle before flying off.

MUSCARELLO'S STORY

Bertrand returned to the Exeter police station at 2.30 a.m. There he found Norman Muscarello, who was shaking with fear. Eventually Bertrand got Muscarello's story out of him.

Muscarello had been walking to Exeter along Route 150 when a group of five red lights came swooping down from the sky to hover over a house. The lights began to pulsate in a repetitive pattern before suddenly darting toward him, causing Muscarello to dive into a ditch. When he looked again, the lights were dropping beyond a line of trees, as if they were landing in the field on the far side.

▲ Were the bright lights that Muscarello saw in fact alien spacecraft?

▲ As they approached the UFO, Patrolman Bertrand drew his gun. However, he did not open fire.

SPOOKY LIGHTS

Bertrand drove Muscarello back to the field where he had seen the lights. They were about 15 m (50 ft) from the car when the cattle at a nearby farm began making alarmed noises. Suddenly the red lights rose up from the ground behind the trees.

Bertrand drew his pistol as the lights came closer but did not fire. The two men hid behind the car as the lights approached to within 30 m (100 ft). Bertrand radioed for backup. By the time Patrolman David Hunt arrived, the red lights had retreated to about 1/2 km (1/3 mi) away. They rose into the sky and headed rapidly away.

Examining The Evidence

Sticking to their story

Bertrand and Hunt made a formal report about the Exeter incident. The Pentagon claimed the men must have mistaken a flight of B-47 military aircraft that had overpassed the area. Bertrand and Hunt pointed out they had spent many nights driving the highways and were familiar with B-47s. In any case, the B-47 flight had passed over around 1.30 a.m. and the sighting had continued until past 3 a.m. Later, the Pentagon agreed to reclassify the sighting as unidentified. The Exeter incident is interesting both because of the number of witnesses and because the police witnesses went to such lengths to defend their story.

MAN IN BLACK

In 1976, Dr. Herbert Hopkins, a doctor and hypnotist, was regularly meeting UFO witness David Stephens to discuss his experience. Hopkins claims that he received a phone call on the evening of September 11 from a man claiming to be vice president of the New Jersey UFO Research Organization. The man asked if he could drop by to discuss the Stephens case. Hopkins agreed.

STRANGE VISITOR
According to Hopkins, the man arrived at his home just moments later. He was dressed in a smart black suit with a black hat, black shoes, black tie, dark gloves, and a white shirt. Hopkins invited the man in and asked him to sit down. The man removed his hat to reveal that he was totally bald. His head and face were pale.

The two men chatted for a while about the Stephens case. Hopkins noticed that his guest spoke in a curiously flat, emotionless monotone. Even stranger, he was wearing lipstick that came off on his glove when he brushed his lips with his fingers.

▲ Was the man in black who visited Herbert Hopkins human or something more sinister?

DISAPPEARING TRICK
Suddenly the man asked Hopkins for a coin. Hopkins says he handed one over and was surprised to see it vanish from the man's open palm. The man then explained he could make a heart vanish from within a human body just as easily. He ordered Hopkins

to stop working on the Stephens case and to destroy all his files. By now terrified, Hopkins agreed.

The man then began to slur his words. He stood abruptly and said, "My energy is running low and I must go now." The man walked with some difficulty out of the house. Outside, Hopkins saw a bright bluish light that he took to be car headlights.

Later, Hopkins found odd marks on his driveway unlike those that would have been left by a car. He discovered there was no such thing as the New Jersey UFO Research Organization. He dropped the Stephens case and destroyed the files.

▲ According to Hopkins, the mysterious man made a coin vanish into his hand.

FACT HUNTER

MEN IN BLACK

- **WHAT ARE THEY?**
"Men in black" are men dressed in black suits who claim to be officials of secret organizations or government agents. They threaten UFO witnesses to keep quiet about what they have seen.

- **HOW DO THEY BEHAVE?**
They usually have detailed information on the people they contact. They are often confused by everyday items such as pens or eating utensils.

- **WHO ARE THEY REALLY?**
Some UFOlogists believe men in black are in fact aliens, or androids controlled by aliens sent out to cover up alien activity on Earth. Others think they are government agents seeking to hush up UFO sightings. A third theory is that they are hallucinations caused by the trauma of encountering a UFO.

FATAL ENCOUNTER AT BASS STRAIT

On the evening of October 21, 1978, 20-year-old pilot Frederick Valentich was flying from Melbourne, Australia, to King Island. He took off in his Cessna 182 at 6.19 p.m. and by 7 p.m. he was flying over Bass Strait, the stretch of sea between Tasmania and mainland Australia.

NEAR MISS

At 7.06 p.m., Valentich radioed Melbourne Flight Control to ask if there were any other aircraft in his area. Melbourne Flight Control replied that no known aircraft were around. There was a slight pause, then Valentich reported over the radio that a large aircraft showing four bright lights had just flown by, about 300 m (1,000 ft) above his own aircraft.

▼ Frederick Valentich reported to Melbourne Flight Control that he had encountered a mysterious craft over Bass Strait.

"IT'S NOT AN AIRCRAFT"

At 7.09 p.m., Valentich reported, "It seems to be playing some sort of game with me." Melbourne asked if he could identify the aircraft. "It's not an aircraft," came the surprising response. "It is flying past. It has a long shape." There was a pause, then he cried, "It's coming for me right now." Then Valentich seemed to calm down. "I'm orbiting and the thing is orbiting on top of me. It has a green light and a sort of metallic light on the outside."

VANISHED

All seemed well until 7:12 p.m. when Valentich came back on the radio to say, "Engine is rough and coughing ... Unknown aircraft is on top of me." There was a burst of static, then silence. Melbourne repeatedly tried contacting Valentich but received no response. At 7.28 p.m., Melbourne ordered a search to begin. No sign of Valentich or his Cessna was ever found.

▼ The lighthouse at Cape Otway, Victoria, overlooking the wild southern seas over which Frederick Valentich's aircraft vanished.

Examining The Evidence

Flying upside down?

Over the weeks following Valentich's disappearance there were many attempts to explain what had happened. One suggestion was that Valentich had somehow turned the aircraft upside down and was seeing the reflection of his own lights in the sea. However, he had the UFO in sight for about seven minutes and the Cessna can fly upside down for only 30 seconds before the fuel system collapses.

THE LIVINGSTON UFO ASSAULT

At 10 a.m. on November 9, 1979, Scottish forestry worker Robert Taylor walked into a forest outside Livingston, Scotland, west of Edinburgh. In a clearing in the forest he encountered a dark, hovering object about 6 m (20 ft) across. It was round with a thin rim around its base.

BLACK SPHERES

According to Taylor's account, he stopped in alarm. Almost at once he saw he was being approached by two black balls coming from the direction of the object. Each one was a little under 1 m (3 ft) in diameter and had six legs on its surface.

The balls rolled toward him on their legs, making soft sucking noises as each leg touched the ground. Before he could retreat, a leg from each sphere grabbed hold of his leg with another soft sucking sound. The balls began dragging Taylor back toward the object. Taylor struggled to free himself. There was now a burning stench so intense he could barely breathe. He felt himself growing dizzy and losing consciousness.

▲ Taylor claimed that he was attacked by two black spheres with spiked legs.

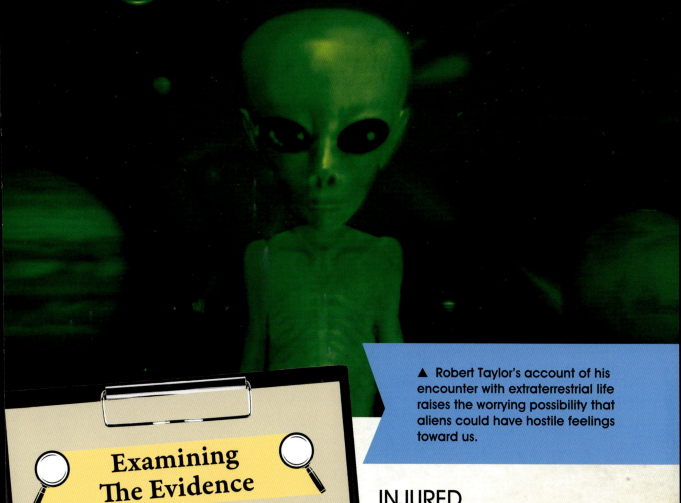

▲ Robert Taylor's account of his encounter with extraterrestrial life raises the worrying possibility that aliens could have hostile feelings toward us.

Examining The Evidence

Marks in the soil

The police went to the clearing and examined marks in the soil. They found two parallel tracks, 2.5 m (8 ft) long and 30 cm (1 ft) wide. These were formed from crushed grass, as if a very heavy weight had rested on them. Around these tracks were two circles of holes driven into the soil. Each hole was circular, about 10 cm (4 in) across and 15 cm (6 in) deep. There were 40 holes in all, driven in at an angle away from the tracks. No heavy machinery had been used in the clearing for months. The police found the marks to be consistent with Taylor's story.

INJURED

Taylor woke up 20 minutes later, lying face down on the grass. The strange objects had gone. Taylor's clothes were torn where the objects had grabbed him. One of his legs was bruised and his chin was bleeding. He couldn't stand and had to crawl back to his truck. When he got home, he called his boss and told him his story.

ALIENS 31

HAUNTINGS

ANCIENT APPARITIONS

The belief in an immortal human soul and its survival after death dates back to prehistoric times and is common to almost every culture around the world.

A WOMAN WRONGED

According to a Japanese folk story, there once lived a samurai who believed his wife had been unfaithful to him. In a jealous rage, he disfigured her, slicing at her face, and said, "Who will think you're beautiful now?"

▲ This eighteenth-century Japanese painting by Maruyama Okyo shows a man terrified when his own ghostly painting comes to life.

BACK FROM THE DEAD

Ever since that day, the spirit of that woman has been found wandering through the fog, her face covered with a mask. She is known as *Kuchisake-onna*, which translates as "Slit-Mouthed Woman." When she meets young men and women, she asks *"Watashi kirei?"* (Am I beautiful?) If they answer "yes" she tears off the mask, revealing the true horror of her face, and asks again. If people keep their nerve and again answer "yes," she allows them to go on their way.

Examining The Evidence

Are ghosts real?

The witnesses whose stories have been told in this chapter were probably telling the truth, and believed they experienced something supernatural. But could their senses have been deceiving them? Sometimes ghostly apparitions can be explained by people seeing unusual reflections or shadows, or hearing strange echoes. Noises below the range of human hearing can make people feel that someone else is in the room with them. Scientists have also suggested that some "haunted" houses may have unusual magnetic fields, which can trigger hallucinations. However, science cannot prove that ghosts definitely do not exist.

By contrast, if they answer truthfully by saying "no," or try to flee from her, *Kuchisake-onna* pursues them, brandishing a scythe. If she catches a man, he's as good as dead. However, if she catches a woman, she may turn her into another *Kuchisake-onna*, doomed to wander the world as a spirit of vengeance.

▼ Many people believe that we have not just a physical body, but also a spiritual body, which can live on after death.

FATEFUL APPEARANCES

According to some stories, ghosts of the recently departed occasionally appear to relatives in order to pass on important messages.

BIBLICAL MESSAGE

In 1925, James Chaffin of Davie County, North Carolina, dreamed that his dead father urged him to look for his missing will in the pocket of the overcoat that he was wearing in the dream. James found the coat with his brother John. In the lining of the inside pocket they found a message in his father's handwriting. It told them to read Genesis 27 in the family Bible. They opened the Bible to the first page of that chapter, and discovered the missing will.

▼ James Chaffin was told to read Chapter 27 of Genesis in the Bible.

▲ This illustration by R. Dunley (published 1856–1858) shows Shakespeare's Hamlet being approached by the ghost of his murdered father.

FATHER'S WARNING

The Society of Psychical Research reported a story about a woman, "Mrs. P.," who one night saw a stranger standing at the foot of her bed, dressed in a naval officer's uniform. She woke her husband. He recognized the intruder as his father, who had died several years earlier. The ghost simply spoke his son's name and walked through the facing wall.

The husband later confessed to his wife that he had accumulated a large debt and was so desperate that he had been thinking of going into business with a dishonest character. He took his father's appearance as a warning and was now determined to solve his financial difficulties by himself.

STRANGE STORIES

GARMENT GIFT

American farmer Michael Conley passed away in 1885. When his daughter was informed of his death, she fainted. On recovering, she claimed that her father had appeared to her and told her to recover a roll of dollar bills he had sewn into the lining of his shirt. She said he'd wrapped the money in a square of red cloth. No one believed her, but they agreed to get the clothes from the morgue. In the lining of the shirt, wrapped in a patch of red cloth, was a roll of dollar bills.

GHOSTS OF WAR

During World War I, both the Germans and the Allies reported several sightings of ghostly soldiers who intervened to save the lives of their comrades.

▲ It was a popular legend by 1914 that a host of angels had helped to repel a German advance in World War I.

SPECTRAL SOLDIER

In November 1916, British soldiers were defending their trench against a German attack when they apparently saw the white figure of a soldier rise out of a shell hole and walk slowly along the front, oblivious to shells and bullets. It then turned toward the Germans, and they scattered in terror.

The same phantom figure was seen later by a British officer, William Speight, in his dugout. It pointed to a spot on the dugout floor, then vanished. Speight ordered a hole to be dug on the spot. To his amazement, the diggers unearthed a tunnel excavated by the Germans, primed with mines timed to explode 13 hours later.

STRANGE STORIES

SAYING GOOD-BYE

World War I soldier and poet Wilfred Owen was killed a week before the war ended. His brother Harold, a naval officer, described his final "meeting" with him on Armistice Day. At the time, Harold didn't know his brother was already dead.

"to my amazement I saw Wilfred sitting in my chair ... I felt shock run through me with appalling force ... I spoke quietly: 'Wilfred how did you get here?' He did not rise and I saw that he was involuntarily immobile, but ... when I spoke his whole face broke into his sweetest and endearing dark smile ... I must have turned my eyes away from him; when I looked back my cabin chair was empty."

▼ Belief in automatic writing was fashionable in Victorian London. Spiritualists believed that a spirit could control a person's writing hand to send a message.

SPOOKY SCRIPT

Sir Arthur Conan Doyle, creator of Sherlock Holmes, had an acquaintance, Lily Loder-Symonds, who believed that spirits could write through her. To Conan Doyle's astonishment, Loder-Symonds one day began writing in the style of his late brother-in-law, Malcolm Leckie, who had been killed at the Battle of Mons in 1915. Conan Doyle asked "Malcolm" questions that he believed only his brother-in-law could have answered. All were answered correctly.

LIVING APPARITIONS

It's a well-known theory that ghosts are the spirits of the dead. But some people believe that living people can also have a ghostly double.

▲ Many people believe that it is possible for living people to appear in one location while they are elsewhere.

TWO PLACES AT ONCE

Emilie Sagee was a teacher at a girls' school in Livonia in 1845. She was capable and conscientious, but there was something odd about her. Stories spread that she was often seen in two parts of the school simultaneously. On one occasion, a class of 13 saw Miss Sagee standing with her doppelgänger at the blackboard.

One morning, the entire school was in a classroom overlooking the garden where Miss Sagee could be seen picking flowers. Suddenly, her double appeared in a chair in the classroom. Outside, her movements grew sluggish. According to witnesses, two of the girls touched the double and their hands passed right through it. Moments later, the double faded,

and Miss Sagee began moving normally again.

PHANTOM FORERUNNER

Businessman Erkson Gorique visited Norway for the first time in July 1955—or did he? When he checked into his hotel, the clerk said: "It's good to have you back, Mr. Gorique." The next day, Gorique introduced himself to a potential customer and was greeted like an old acquaintance. Mystified, Gorique assured the man it was his first visit. The customer just smiled. "This is not so unusual here in Norway," he said. "In fact, it happens so often we have a name for it. We call it the *vardoger*, or forerunner."

STRANGE STORIES

SAVE OUR SOULS

In 1828, the first mate of a cargo ship off the Canadian coast found a stranger in the captain's cabin busy writing a message on a slate. The stranger then disappeared. His message read: "Steer to the nor'west." The captain did so and soon they came upon a sinking vessel damaged by an iceberg. Among the rescued crew was a man identical to the phantom. When questioned, he admitted dreaming of going aboard this very ship to request help.

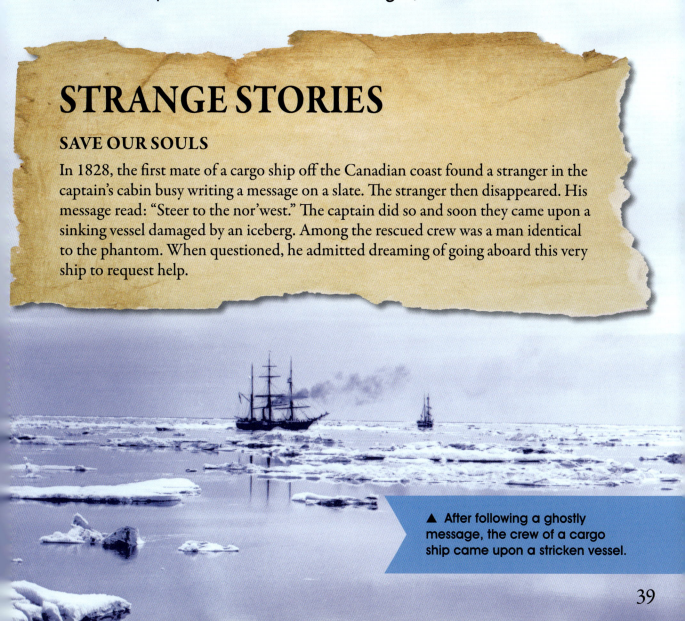

▲ After following a ghostly message, the crew of a cargo ship came upon a stricken vessel.

TALKING TO THE DEAD

Psychic mediums claim to have a heightened sensitivity to the subtle forces and presences around us. This, they say, enables them to act as a channel between the living and the dead.

BETTY SHINE

Celebrity psychic Betty Shine said that she obtained her "powers" in an unusual way. As a young evacuee during World War II, her house was struck by a stray bomb, which blew in the windows and sent a shard of glass into the headboard just above her head. The following night, Betty began seeing "misty people" passing through the room. She soon realized that they were spirits of the dead, which she could now see.

▼ Séances are attempts by living people to contact the spirits of the dead.

▶ Some religious people believe that using Ouija boards can be dangerous.

TINA HAMILTON

Tina Hamilton is a Catholic sacristan (an officer of the Church) who lives in Canterbury, England. She says that she often senses the presence of spirits. Once she says that she encountered the confused spirit of a young man who had been killed in a car accident. She said he kept reliving the crash like a bad dream and couldn't accept he hadn't survived.

MYSTERY BELL

Psychic John Edward says that messages can be hard to interpret. One male spirit kept showing him a bell. What could it mean? The man's bereaved wife said that just before his death, her husband had given her a souvenir bell as a gift, and that it was proof that the spirit was real.

FACT HUNTER

OUIJA BOARD

- **WHAT IS IT?**

A board printed with letters, to which a planchette (movable indicator) points, to allow communication with the dead. It was popularized by the Fuld brothers of Baltimore in 1898.

- **HOW DOES IT WORK?**

Participants place their finger on the planchette and wait for spirits to move it to spell out answers to their questions.

- **POSSIBLE EXPLANATION**

Involuntary muscle contractions in participants' hands known as ideomotor actions.

POSSESSION

Some people believe that dead souls can take over the bodies of the living. It sounds scary, but they say it can be for a benign purpose, as in the case of Lurancy Vennum.

THE VENNUM CASE

At the age of 13, Lurancy Vennum from Watseka, Illinois, fell into a trance during which she claimed to be Mary Roff, a local girl who had died when Lurancy was a year old. She asked if she could go "home," and the Roffs agreed to take her in. Lurancy as "Mary" recognized the furnishings in the house, and identified many of Mary's prized possessions. She even greeted Mary's old Sunday school teacher by name. She was able to answer many personal questions thrown at her by the Roffs, including details of a family holiday and where a pet dog had died.

▲ Lurancy appeared to be taken over completely by the spirit of "Mary."

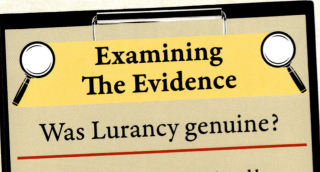

Examining The Evidence

Was Lurancy genuine?

The Lurancy case was reviewed by psychologist Frank Hoffmann. He said that the grieving Roff family encouraged Lurancy to believe that she was Mary. Another investigator, Henry Bruce, pointed out that the "Mary personality" only appeared when the Roffs were present and disappeared entirely upon Lurancy's marriage.

RETURNING SPIRITS

John and Florence Pollock were heartbroken when their daughters, Joanna and Jacqueline, were killed in a car crash in Hexham, England, in 1957. Two years later, Florence gave birth to twin girls. The girls grew up in a different town, but when they were three they were taken back to Hexham. The girls recognized the family's former home, the school, and places where their sisters used to play. At age four, they were given their dead sisters' toy box and could identify all the dolls by name. Disturbingly, they seemed to remember being run over by a car. Their parents had never told them about the accident. Were they reincarnations of their sisters? Some, including their father, were sure of it.

▼ A priest tries to drive out a spirit in a scene from the 1973 movie *The Exorcist*.

THE BLOODY TOWER

If any site deserves its reputation for spectral sightings, it is the Tower of London, whose weathered stones are soaked in the blood of countless executed martyrs and traitors.

THE TWO PRINCES

In 1483, Princes Edward and Richard of England may have been murdered by their ambitious uncle, the Duke of Gloucester, who became King of England, Richard III, that same year. No one knows the truth, but the two boys have been seen on several occasions, walking through the tower's chilly corridors at dusk.

GHOSTLY PURSUIT

The Countess of Salisbury, Margaret Pole, was 70 years old when she was condemned to death for treason in 1541. Standing regally on the scaffold, she refused to kneel for the executioner. Instead, she commanded him to sever her head where she stood. When he refused, she fled, and was killed after a bloody chase.

▼ The Tower of London on the River Thames.

It is said that after dark, on the anniversary of her death, this gruesome scene is reenacted, as Pole's ghost tries once again to outrun her executioner.

THE PHANTOM QUEEN

Lady Jane Grey was just 15 years old when she became queen in 1553. She ruled for only nine days, before being arrested and condemned to death. She was beheaded on Tower Hill on February 12, 1554. Since then, her ghost has been seen by witnesses on several occasions. In 1957, two sentries swore they witnessed the apparition of the young queen on the roof of the Salt Tower.

▲ Does the ghost of Anne Boleyn still roam the Tower of London today?

STRANGE STORIES

ANNE BOLEYN

Anne Boleyn, the second wife of Henry VIII, was beheaded in 1536. Startled visitors have reported seeing her lead a spectral procession through the Tower Chapel, where she made her final prayers, sometimes with and sometimes without her head.

THE GHOSTS OF GLAMIS

Glamis Castle in Scotland is the ancestral home of the late Queen Mother, born Elizabeth Bowes-Lyon. It also has the unenviable reputation as the most haunted castle in the world.

CASTLE LEGENDS

Several visitors claim to have seen a pale, frightened young girl pleading in mute terror at a barred window. Legend has it she had her tongue cut out for betraying a family secret.

In 1537, the widow of the sixth Lord Glamis was burned for witchcraft. It is said that ever since, on the anniversary of her death, her ghost has been seen on the roof of the clock tower, bathed in an eerie red glow.

In the 1920s, a workman was said to have accidentally uncovered a hidden passage and to have been driven to the edge of insanity by what he found there. Allegedly the family bought his silence by paying for him to relocate to another country.

▼ Glamis Castle is said to be home to several ghosts.

GHOSTLY FIGURE

In 1869, a guest named Mrs. Munro was awoken in the night by the sensation of someone bending over her. She may even have felt a beard brush her face. The night-light had gone out, so she told her husband to get up and find the matches. In the moonlight, she saw a figure pass into the dressing room. Creeping to the end of the bed, she felt for and found the matchbox.

She lit a match and called out loudly, "Cam, Cam, I've found the matches." To her surprise she saw that her husband hadn't moved from her side. There was no one in the room.

▲ A man appears to be startled by a white-garbed ghost in this photograph from 1910.

EYEWITNESS TO MYSTERY

DEATH'S DOOR

Scottish novelist Sir Walter Scott braved a night at Glamis Castle in 1793 and regretted it. He said, "I must own, that when I heard door after door shut, after my conductor had retired, I began to consider myself as too far from the living, and somewhat too near the dead."

NOISES IN THE NIGHT

During the spring of 1848, the Fox family of Hydesville, New York, claimed that their nights were disturbed by strange noises. The family slept in the same room, so all claimed to hear the noises.

COMMUNICATING WITH THE DEAD

On the evening of March 31, Mrs. Fox and her children Margaretta and Kate were in bed when they heard a loud rapping. Kate assumed someone was playing a practical joke. She challenged whomever it was to copy her. She snapped her fingers and was immediately answered by the same number of raps.

Mrs. Fox asked out loud if it was a human being making the noises. There was no reply. "Is it a spirit?" she asked. "If it is, make two raps." She was answered emphatically with two loud bangs that shook the whole house.

▼ The Fox family responding to mysterious rappings in their home in Hydesville, New York, as illustrated in literature of the time.

MURDER MOST FOUL

Mrs. Fox developed a simple code to communicate with the spirit, and the intruder (so she claimed) told her that it was the spirit of a 31-year-old man who had been murdered in the house. A nearby resident named William Duesler was invited into the room. Using Mrs. Fox's code, Duesler discovered that the murdered man was a salesman named Charles Rosma, who had been killed five years earlier by a previous tenant of the house, a Mr. Bell, for the $500 he had saved and carried with him.

▲ The Fox sisters Margaretta (left) and Kate (middle) with their older sister, Leah, who had left home at the time of the haunting.

When the murdered man informed the family that his body had been buried in their cellar, Mr. Fox started digging up the dirt floor. He discovered human bone fragments 1.5 m (5 ft) down.

EYEWITNESS TO MYSTERY

TESTING THE TAPPER

Mrs. Fox later wrote: "I then thought I could put a test that no one in the place could answer. I asked the noise to rap my different children's ages, successively. Instantly, each one of my children's ages was given correctly."

TOMBSTONE

They called Tombstone, Arizona, the town too tough to die and, according to the stories, some of its most notorious inhabitants are equally reluctant to go quietly.

GHOST TOWN

The town is now preserved as a national museum and many of the old buildings have been restored to their former rickety glory. Some say that if you stay in the bar after closing time, you can hear the honky-tonk piano playing "Red River Valley" and hear the cowboys' raucous laughter.

SALOON GHOSTS

The meanest gunfighters of the Old West once drank and gambled at the town's Bird Cage Theater, which doubled as a saloon. According to tour guides, 31 ghosts haunt the saloon, which was the site of 26 killings.

The phantom most frequently seen is a stagehand dressed in black striped clothing.

▼ This photo of Tombstone dates from 1885. The town suffered two major fires in 1881 and 1882. By the mid-1880s, the place was virtually abandoned.

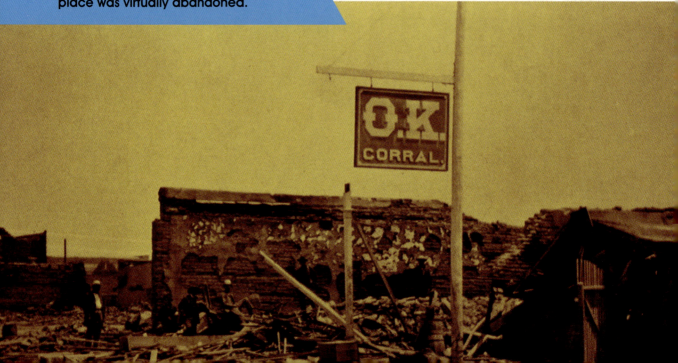

▶ Violent deaths were not uncommon in the Old West.

WOMAN IN WHITE

Saloon staff say that objects such as poker chips regularly appear and disappear, and furniture moves by itself. One member of staff said he was physically attacked by a spirit. A woman working in the gift store swears she once saw on a security monitor a woman in a white dress walking through the cellar.

STRANGE STORIES

THE GHOST OF BOOT HILL CEMETERY

In 1996, Terry Ike Clanton took a photo of his friend at Tombstone's cemetery on Boot Hill. When Clanton had the photo developed, he was startled to see among the gravestones, just to the right of his friend, a thin man in a dark hat. The man appears to be legless and kneeling or rising up out of the ground. Clanton is confident there was no one else in the shot when he took the photo. Unlike Clanton's friend, the man casts no shadow.

BORLEY RECTORY

During the 1930s and 1940s, Borley Rectory became known as the most haunted house in England. This vicarage near Sudbury, Essex, was built on the site of a monastery. It is said that a Borley monk fell in love with a local nun. They were caught together, and the monk was executed. The nun was walled up alive in the cellar.

FIRST SIGHTINGS

The first resident of the new rectory was the Reverend Bull, who often observed the weeping nun wandering his garden in search of her lost love.

▼ Bones were found in the cellar of the rectory and, in an effort to quiet the ghost, given a decent burial in Liston churchyard in 1945.

◀ The ruins of Borley Rectory at the start of its demolition. A brick flies through the air (circled below). Is this a paranormal event captured on film?

GHOST HUNTER

In 1929, Reverend Eric Smith and his wife moved in and were immediately confronted by poltergeist activity. They decided to call in a ghost hunter, Harry Price. He recorded incidents involving phantom footsteps, flying objects, and even physical attacks. Unintelligible messages were scrawled on the walls, servants' bells rang of their own accord, and music could be heard coming from the chapel while it was empty.

BURNED DOWN

The Smiths left after just two years, and their successors did not last much longer. The house burned down in a mysterious fire in 1939.

Examining The Evidence

Did Price fake the evidence?

Harry Price made his name with a best-selling book about Borley, but some people raised questions. They said that Price, a former stage magician, faked certain phenomena. Yet the Bull family claimed the house was haunted before Price moved in. Even if Price were a fraud, it seems that there may have been something genuinely mysterious going on at Borley Rectory.

ALCATRAZ

Long before Alcatraz Island in San Francisco Bay was converted into a prison, Native Americans warned the U.S. Army not to build a fortress on what was called the Rock, as it was the dwelling place of evil spirits.

DEMON EYES

When the fortress was converted into a military prison in 1912, several soldiers were said to have been driven insane by mysterious noises in the night, by cold spots that turned their breath to mist, and by the sight of burning red eyes that appeared in the lower-level cells.

Even the most hardened inmates feared being thrown into "the hole," the windowless cells of D Block where the red-eyed demon was said to dwell.

▼ According to Native American beliefs, the Rock was the dwelling place of evil spirits, and anyone living there was in peril.

▼ Various parts of the prison are said to be haunted by the ghosts of inmates who died while attempting to escape, or else died by suicide or were murdered.

STRANGE STORIES

MYSTERY OF 14D

On one memorable night during the 1940s, a prisoner was hurled screaming into solitary confinement in 14D and continued yelling all night. When the guards finally opened his cell, they found him dead, with distinctive marks around his throat. The official cause of death was given as "non-self-inflicted strangulation."

The next morning, the prisoners were lined up for roll call, but the number was wrong. There was one extra prisoner in the line. A guard walked along the line to see if an inmate was playing a trick on him. He later claimed that he came face-to-face with the dead man, who promptly vanished before his eyes.

JAILHOUSE JITTERS

The ghosts of prisoners who died attempting to escape are said to haunt the hospital block where their bodies were taken. Other parts of the prison are host to the unquiet spirits of the five suicides and eight murders that took place before the prison was closed in 1963.

Since the Rock opened to tourists, visitors have claimed to have heard the sound of sobbing, moaning, and phantom footsteps.

HAUNTINGS 55

WHAT WAS ATLANTIS?

According to legend, Atlantis was a beautiful, rich, and powerful island nation. It was described by the ancient Greek philosopher Plato in about 360 BCE as lying "beyond the Pillars of Heracles" (the Straits of Gibraltar). However, according to Plato, in the middle of a war between Atlantis and Mediterranean countries in 9000 BCE, the island sank into the sea in a single day and night.

▲ This is an artist's impression of the architecture of Atlantis, with a great temple rising above the rest of the city.

IMPERIAL CITY

According to Plato, the island of Atlantis was mountainous and lushly forested. South of Mount Atlas, its towering dormant volcano, was a fertile plain irrigated by a network of canals. South of the plain was the city of Atlantis, capital of a mighty oceanic empire.

The city of Atlantis, Plato records, was composed of circles within circles of land and water connected by bridged canals. Each artificial island was surrounded by high walls and mighty watchtowers.

The smallest central island contained the imperial palace and a magnificent

◀ Plato claimed that the citizens of Atlantis worshipped the sea god Poseidon.

of the other rulers on any complaint made against them. This was because Poseidon's laws forbade the kings from making war on each other, and required them to stand together and take united action against any external enemy.

temple of the sea god Poseidon, legendary founder of Atlantis.

RULERS OF ATLANTIS

Plato explains that the empire was governed by ten kings, all directly descended from the sea god. The kings had absolute power over their cities and regions. However, they accepted the verdict

Examining The Evidence

Did Atlantis exist?

The legend of Atlantis has been a source of fascination since it was rediscovered by scholars in the seventeenth century. But did the island ever exist? Atlantologists (seekers of Atlantis) argue that a large landmass may once have existed in the location of the Mid-Atlantic Ridge, which certainly suffers from earthquakes and volcanoes. However, most Plato scholars believe that his Atlantis was imaginary. Plato's story could have been inspired by the fate of the island of Santorini in the Mediterranean. Santorini was destroyed by a volcanic eruption in about 1600 BCE.

LOST LANDS

WHAT WAS LEMURIA?

Lemuria, or Mu, is a lost island said to have existed long ago in the Pacific Ocean. In 1864, zoologist Philip Sclater realized that fossils of lemurs were found on Madagascar (an island off Africa) as well as India. He proposed that both countries were once part of a larger continent, which he named Lemuria.

PACIFIC CULTURE

The idea of the lost continent of Lemuria was picked up by nineteenth-century believers in supernatural phenomena, such as Helena Blavatsky, William Scott-Elliot, and James Bramwell. According to their theories, Mu was a culture that spread its influence over many Pacific islands before it was swallowed up by the ocean. Forced to abandon their homes, the Lemurians settled in Melanesia and Polynesia. Some moved to Central and South America.

▼ Could the monumental, sculpted heads of the Olmecs in Mexico have been influenced by Lemurian culture?

Examining The Evidence

Did Lemuria exist?

The mainstream scientific community no longer believes that Lemuria existed. According to the theory of plate tectonics, accepted now by all geologists, Madagascar and India were indeed once part of the same landmass, but plate movement caused India to break away millions of years ago and move to its present location. The original landmass very slowly broke apart. It did not sink beneath the sea.

▼ According to some, the statues of Easter Island are evidence of the existence of Lemuria.

SPIRITUAL EMPIRE

Blavatsky and her colleagues believed that Mu existed at the same time as Atlantis. However, they said, the two civilizations were very different. While Atlantis was a technologically advanced and warlike culture, the Lemurians were a simple, seafaring people. They sailed to other parts of the world to spread their spiritual beliefs. They built ceremonial hubs, sacred sculptures, and roads. Mu's influence, they said, can be seen in statues such as the colossi of Easter Island.

SEEKERS OF ATLANTIS

Following the collapse of ancient Greek and Roman civilization, Plato's story of Atlantis was dismissed and forgotten. However, this story of a lost island was revived in the seventeenth century by the German Jesuit priest Athanasius Kircher.

KIRCHER'S MAP

Kircher was the first scholar to seriously study the Atlantis legend. His research led him to the immense collection of ancient sources at the Vatican Library. Here he came across a well-preserved leather map of Atlantis. The map had come to Rome from Egypt in the first century CE, but Kircher believed it had been made in the fourth century BCE, during Plato's time.

The map shows Atlantis as a large island. It depicts a high, centrally located volcano, most likely representing Mount Atlas, along with six major rivers.

▲ This map of Atlantis was found in the Vatican Library by Athanasius Kircher. Does it show a real place?

RUDBECK

Olaus Rudbeck (1630–1702) was a Swedish professor of medicine and amateur archaeologist who found evidence for Atlantis through excavations and research in his own country. He claimed that Norse myths and archaeological evidence proved that some

60 LOST LANDS

DONNELLY AND BERLITZ

The man most responsible for bringing Atlantis to the attention of the wider public was Ignatius Donnelly (1831–1901), a U.S. Congressman and founder of Atlantology. Donnelly's 1882 book, *Atlantis, the Antediluvian World*, was a runaway bestseller and is still published in more than a dozen languages.

The work of popularizing Atlantis further was later taken up by Charles Berlitz (1913–2003). A talented linguist, teacher, and writer, Berlitz concluded that many modern and ancient languages derive from a single prehistoric source, which he argued could be traced to Atlantis.

▲ U.S. Congressman Ignatius Donnelly was adamant in his belief that Atlantis really existed.

survivors from Atlantis had come to Sweden. Their influence, he said, led to the rise of the Vikings.

EYEWITNESS TO MYSTERY

IMMORTAL PINNACLES

The poet William Blake (1757–1827) was inspired by the legend of Atlantis to write: "On those vast shady hills between America and Albion's shore, Now barr'd out by the Atlantic sea, call'd Atlantean hills, Because from their bright summits you may pass to the Golden World, An ancient palace, archetype of mighty Emperies, Rears its immortal pinnacles …"

LOST LANDS

TECHNOLOGY OF ATLANTIS

According to Atlantologists, the great, lost civilization was incredibly technologically advanced. The citizens of Atlantis, so Atlantologists claim, mastered flight many millennia before the invention of the plane by the Wright brothers.

ANCIENT AVIATORS?

At the end of the nineteenth century, an ancient wooden object that looked exactly like a model airplane was excavated in the Upper Nile Valley. Ancient Hindu sources refer to aircraft called *vimanas*. The Incas told stories of an age-old hero called Kon-Tiki Viracocha, who rose high into the air aboard a flying temple. In southwestern North America, the Hopi Indians spoke of *pauwvotas*, airborne vehicles flown over immense distances by an ancestral people before their island perished during the Great Deluge. Atlantologists theorize that these folk memories are all that remain of a lost Atlantean supertechnology that created some kind of aircraft.

▲ Could the flying temples of the Hindu scriptures have been inspired by real Atlantean technology?

BUILDERS AND MINERS

One area in which Atlantologists believe the Atlanteans excelled was building. The Great Pyramid is the oldest of the Egyptian pyramids. From whom did the Egyptians acquire these building skills? The Egyptians record that Thaut,

EYEWITNESS TO MYSTERY

PLATO DESCRIBES THE WALLS OF ATLANTIS

"The entire circuit of the wall which went around the outermost one they covered with a coating of brass, and the circuit of the next wall they coated with tin, and the third, which encompassed the citadel, flashed with the red light of orichalcum (high-grade copper)."

survivor of the flood that brought his fellow "followers of Horus" to the Nile Delta, was the Great Pyramid's chief architect.

The Menominee Indians of North America's Upper Great Lakes region tell of the marine men, white-skinned people from across the Atlantic who dug out Mother Earth's shiny bones. This is a reference to copper miners who excavated the land in the region between 3100 BCE and 1200 BCE. The miners used "magical stones," which the Indians called *yuwipi*, to locate the underground veins of copper. Could the pale-faced foreigners have been Atlanteans using their mining skills in North America?

◀ Some authors have claimed that the pyramids were built by Atlanteans to transform seismic (earthquake) energy into electricity.

HOW WERE ATLANTIS AND LEMURIA DESTROYED?

The French astronomer G.R. Carli was the first person to conclude, in 1785, that Atlantis was destroyed by a comet colliding with the Earth. Dismissed at the time, the idea was revived in the 1930s by Austrian engineer Hans Hoerbiger, who blamed the impact of a fragment of frozen comet for the catastrophe. In 1964, German engineer Otto Muck found twin deep-sea holes in the Atlantic floor. He claimed these were caused by an asteroid that set off a chain reaction of subsurface volcanoes along the Mid-Atlantic Ridge.

▶ It would have taken a truly huge disaster to obliterate Atlantis so completely.

ATLANTIS—COMETS AND ASTEROIDS

Atlantologists point to two major cometary impacts that could have destroyed Atlantis, in about 2200 BCE and in 1198 BCE. This seems to agree with historical records. Plato and the Roman scholar Varro wrote of floods occurring around 2200 BCE. The Chinese myth of ten suns falling from the sky has also been dated to around then.

Atlantologists believe that Atlantis may have survived the 2200 BCE disaster, but that its final demise came with the bigger catastrophe of 1198 BCE, which brought an end to the Bronze Age. Geologists estimate that asteroids struck the eastern North Atlantic in that year, with global effects. This is reflected in writings of the time.

LEMURIA—VOLCANOES AND TSUNAMIS

A series of geological upheavals appear to have brought great destruction to the Pacific during the late seventeenth century BCE. At that time, Japan's Mount Sanbe and Alaska's Mount Aniakchak erupted, spewing ash into the atmosphere. During the same period, Rabaul in the South Pacific and Hawaii's Mauna Kea exploded. Could the combined effects of these eruptions have been sufficient to destroy Lemuria, if it existed?

STRANGE STORIES

"THE WAVES UPROSE"

Polynesian myth recalls the destruction of Marae Renga, a legendary "land of the Sun." "Uvoke lifted the land with his crowbar. The waves uprose, the country became small ... The waves broke, the wind blew, rain fell, thunder roared ... The king saw that the land had sunk in the sea." Hotu Matua, who led survivors to Easter Island, lamented, "The sea has come up and drowned all people in Marae Renga."

LEGACY OF ATLANTIS: NORTH AFRICA AND EUROPE

In about 3100 BCE, Egypt began its swift rise from a simple farming society to a sophisticated civilization that built temples, developed a written language, and excelled in science, engineering, and the arts. Atlantologists have argued that this transformation came about due to the arrival of Atlantean refugees in the Nile Valley, following the destruction of their homeland.

PAINTINGS AND MYTHS

Atlantologists offer different kinds of evidence to support this argument. For example, they point to the Egyptian myth of Thaut.

Thaut, it is said, arrived in Egypt at the dawn of their civilization bearing tablets of knowledge. He was fleeing a flood that overwhelmed his homeland.

▲ Atlantologists argue that the progress of Egyptian civilization accelerated after it came into contact with Atlantis.

▲ Some writers have claimed that the man in this Egyptian ceramic is an Atlantean prisoner.

FLIGHT TO SPAIN

Near the southern Spanish city of Jaén are the remains of an ancient city laid out in concentric circles of canals and land rings, just as Plato described Atlantis. Could there have been a wave of immigration from Atlantis to Spain?

BASQUES

Farther north, the Basques of the Pyrenees speak of their prehistoric forefathers as inhabitants of Atlaintika. They were said to have sailed from the "Green Isle," a powerful seafaring nation that sank into the Atlantic. The Basque language, Euskara, is unrelated to any Indo-European tongue, but shares similarities with the language of the Guanches, natives of the Canary Islands, and Nahuatl, the language of the Aztecs. All this, Atlantologists say, suggests a link between these peoples and Atlantean culture.

STRANGE STORIES

DOG WORSHIPPERS

The Canary Islands got their name from the Romans because of their custom of dog worship. *Canis* is Latin for "dog." Atlantologists see a link between this and the ancient Egyptian cult of Anubis, the dog-headed god. Both peoples, according to Atlantologists, were descended from the Atlanteans.

LOST LANDS 67

LEGACY OF ATLANTIS: THE AMERICAS

Just as was true for the Egyptians, the rise of civilization in Central America was swift, with the emergence of the Olmecs in about 1250 BCE. Atlantologists believe Atlanteans and Lemurians may have helped in the development of Olmec culture.

MAYA AND AZTECS

According to Mayan tradition, the Maya's first city, Mayapan, was founded by Chumael-Ah-Canule, the "First after the Flood." He escaped the Hun Yecil, the "drowning of the trees," that engulfed his island kingdom across the Atlantic Ocean. The temple frieze at the Mayan city of Tikal begins with the image of a man rowing his boat away from an island city tumbling into the sea during a volcanic eruption.

The Aztecs, a later culture, claimed ancestral descent from the lost volcanic island kingdom of Aztlan in the Atlantic Ocean.

▲ Was the architecture of Tikal influenced by Atlantean ideas?

▲ This Chibcha Indian artwork shows the "Gilded Man," their founding father who arrived from across the sea. Some claim that he was a survivor of Atlantis.

NORTH AMERICA

Tribal myths also seem to point to a lost Atlantean heritage. The O-keepa ceremony of the Mandan Indians in the Dakotas is an annual commemoration of the Great Flood. Mandans paint their skin white to mimic their ancestors who arrived from across the Atlantic.

According to James Churchward, a writer on the Mu, evidence of a Lemurian presence in North America can be found in the Hopi sand paintings of swastikas. This hooked cross, known in Buddhism as the *sauvastika*, is a common image in Asia. Churchward believed that the Asians and ancient Americans may have received this symbol from a common source: Lemuria.

STRANGE STORIES

TALES FROM SOUTH AMERICA

The indigenous peoples of South America have myths that seem to fit in with the Atlantean legend. The Chibchas of Colombia tell of their founder, Muiscas-Zuhe, who came from an island in the Atlantic after it was overwhelmed by a great flood. The Ge-speaking Indians of Brazil speak of King Mai-Ra, who set his island on fire, then sank it beneath the sea, because of its people's immoral conduct. He then sailed to South America with a small band of companions chosen for their virtue.

THE SEARCH FOR ATLANTIS: THE NORTHEAST ATLANTIC

In 1949, Dr. Maurice Ewing, aboard the research vessel *Glomar Challenger*, found an ocean-floor formation in the Northeast Atlantic, later dubbed the Horseshoe Seamounts. It was made up of a large mound ringed by a range of mountains. Its highest peak was a volcano that had collapsed beneath the sea in the past 12,000 years. Could this have been the large island surrounded by a ring of mountains described by Plato?

◀ According to Plato's writings, "There was [on the island of Atlantis] every kind of animal, domesticated and wild, among them numerous elephants."

In 1974, cameras aboard the Soviet research vessel *Academician Petrovsky* captured a series of images resembling the partial remains of human-made ruins. Most appeared around the peak of Mount Ampère, around 65 m (213 ft) below the surface.

▲ This map show the ocean floor in the Atlantic. Off the coast of Portugal can be seen a ring of mountains matching Plato's description of Atlantis.

FACT HUNTER

THE HORSESHOE SEAMOUNTS

- **COULD THIS BE THE SITE OF ATLANTIS?**
The island's estimated dimensions seem similar to those given by Plato. Mount Ampère stands to the south—the same position assumed by Mount Atlas in Plato's description.

- **SO WHY HASN'T ATLANTIS BEEN FOUND YET?**
If a ruined city does exist on Mount Ampère, it will be under many layers of silt, mud, and possibly lava rock. No device currently available is capable of penetrating such thickly layered obstacles.

- **AND IF WE DO PENETRATE THE SILT, WHAT WILL WE FIND?**
Probably very little. Even if Atlantis is down there, the cataclysm that destroyed it, if powerful enough to sink an entire island, is unlikely to have left much in the way of cultural evidence.

BEACH SAND AND ELEPHANT BONES

Expeditions to the undersea mound have retrieved freshwater sand, algae, and rocks that had been formed on dry land, all of which suggested that it had once been an island. Even elephant bones have been dredged from the area, seeming to tie in with Plato's story that these creatures had inhabited Atlantis.

LOST LANDS

THE SEARCH FOR ATLANTIS: THE CARIBBEAN

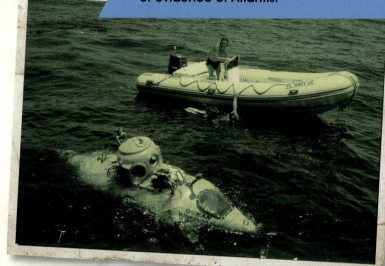

▼ A deep-sea submarine equipped with state-of-the-art equipment dives into the seas around Bimini in search of evidence of Atlantis.

In March 2003, amateur explorers Greg and Lora Little were swimming off the island of Andros in the Caribbean when they came across what appeared to be a giant underwater platform made of three tiers of massive stone blocks.

ANDROS PLATFORM

The platform was 458 m (1,502 ft) long and 50 m (164 ft) wide. Its regular appearance and square-cut blocks suggested it could have been a dock or port of some kind. But what ancient civilization could have built such a massive structure at a time when the area now covered by ocean was dry land? Over the following years, more discoveries were made in the area, including a long stone wall 10 km (6 mi) north of the island. Atlantologists believe this could have been a western outpost of the Atlantean Empire.

THE BIMINI ROAD

The Bimini Road is an underwater rock formation near the island of Bimini in the Bahamas. The structure is made up of huge square blocks that run in two straight lines across the sea bottom

72 LOST LANDS

◀ Atlantis researcher Vonda Osman with a block of stone removed from the Bimini Wall.

stone perfectly fitted together. They argue that the two structures were made by the same Atlantean civilization.

for about 635 m (2,083 ft). The road contains what appear to be several angular keystones with notches to join them together. This is similar to a prehistoric building style encountered in the Andean walls of Cuzco and Machu Picchu. Atlantologists also compared the Bimini Road to the ancient wall of Lixus on the Atlantic coast of Morocco, which is made of huge blocks of square, unmortared

Examining The Evidence

Is the Bimini Road natural or human-made?

Most conventional geologists believe the Bimini Road is a natural feature composed of beachrock that has broken up into a variety of shaped blocks. They say it is a peculiar result of natural processes that can also be found in other parts of the world, including the Tessellated Pavement at Eaglehawk Neck, Tasmania. Atlantologists dispute this. They say that at the time of its formation, the Bimini Road stood well above sea level, so no wave erosion would have been possible. They also point to samples revealing fragments of granite, which is not found elsewhere in the Bahamas.

THE SEARCH FOR LEMURIA

In 1985, a Japanese scuba instructor was diving in the waters off Yonaguni, an island in Japan's Okinawa island chain. The diver found himself facing what appeared to be a great stone building. The photographs he took of the structure sparked national interest. Archaeologists examined the photographs, but could not agree if the structure was natural or human-made.

▶ This is an artist's rendering of the sunken monument lying in the waters off the Japanese island of Yonaguni.

UNDERWATER CITY?

The following year, another diver in Okinawa waters was shocked to discover what looked like a massive underwater arch, perhaps a gateway, of huge stone blocks. They were beautifully fitted together in the manner of prehistoric masonry. This sparked another surge of interest, and by the end of 1986, five more apparently human-made structures were found near three Japanese islands. The formations seemed to be made up of paved streets and crossroads, altar-like formations, grand staircases leading to plazas, and processional ways topped by pairs of towering features resembling pylons. So far, no internal passages or chambers have been found.

If these structures are human-made, who could have built them? Some people claim these are the remains of the lost world of Lemuria. The Lemurians, they say, were either overwhelmed by rising sea levels or the land on which they built these structures gradually collapsed.

SPIRAL STAIRCASE

In 1998, divers found yet another seemingly human-made underwater ruin near the islet of Okinoshima, more than 966 km (600 mi) from Okinawa. It was a row of four round stone towers, each one 7–10 m (23–33 ft) across and almost 30 m (100 ft) high. One of these stone towers featured a spiral staircase winding around the outside.

EYEWITNESS TO MYSTERY

DESCRIBING OKINOSHIMA

Professor Nobuhiro Yoshida says, "Comparing these linear steps, so perfectly suited to anyone climbing them, with the immediate subsurface environment, we notice at once that the sea bottom is otherwise composed exclusively of irregular, round boulders … and therefore in sharp contrast to the vertical columns and rising staircase."

LOST WORLDS OF THE AMERICAS

Atlantis and Lemuria may be the most famous lost civilizations, but there are other phantom realms that play roles in the mythology of different peoples. The lure of these fabled worlds, and the riches they may contain, have tempted many explorers to try and find them.

EL DORADO

Invading Spaniards in the early sixteenth century observed Colombia's Chibcha Indians performing the Guatavita ceremony. This ceremony was to revere their forefather, a legendary golden king. The Spanish convinced themselves the king's city, El Dorado, still existed somewhere in the Colombian interior, and they spent several fruitless centuries searching for it.

SEVEN CITIES OF GOLD

In 1150 CE, as the Moors besieged the city of Mérida in Spain, seven

▲ The Spanish conquistador Coronado mounted an expedition in search of the legendary Seven Cities, but they forever eluded his grasp.

bishops and their congregations fled across the Atlantic by ship. It was reported that they landed on another continent, where they built seven cities, rich in gold and precious stones.

The legend of Cíbola, as the seven cities became known, persisted, and when the Spanish conquered Mexico in 1519, they were eager

76 *LOST LANDS*

caves," and the Spanish interpreted that to mean Cíbola. Unfortunately for them, the legendary seven cities were never found.

CITY OF THE CAESARS

A myth tells that ancient Roman sailors, fleeing civil unrest following Julius Caesar's assassination, were shipwrecked on the southern tip of South America. The story went that the Romans used their expertise to build the Incas an extensive road network, and the native population was so grateful they showered them with gold, silver, and diamonds. The Romans then went on to build a fabulously wealthy city in Patagonia.

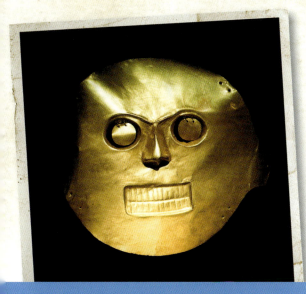

▲ A ceremonial Colombian gold mask. European explorers became convinced that the city of El Dorado contained countless such treasures.

to find it. The Aztec emperor Moctezuma II told them of a place to the north called Chicomoztoc, meaning "place of the seven

STRANGE STORIES

DID THE ROMANS REALLY REACH SOUTH AMERICA?

The City of the Caesars was never found, but intriguing discoveries have been made that suggest the Romans may well have reached South America. From a shipwreck found off Rio de Janeiro, Brazil, in 1976, Roman amphorae (storage jars) were retrieved, and identified as dating from around 250 CE. Bricks used to build the Maya city of Comalcalco were found stamped with Roman mason marks from the second century CE.

LOST WORLDS OF THE NORTH

The icy northern regions of the Earth have always exerted a fascination on people, both ancient and modern, and they have often been the subject of story and myth.

HYPERBOREA

In Greek mythology, Hyperborea, meaning "beyond the north wind," was a mythical land existing far to the north. In this perfect place, the Greeks said, the sun shone for 24 hours a day. In this they were not far from the truth. Beyond the Arctic Circle, the sun does shine for 24 hours a day for a few months during the summer. According to the ancient Greeks, the Hyperboreans were sun worshippers.

Some modern researchers have speculated that Hyperborea could have in fact been Great Britain. The description of the Hyperboreans' great temple seems similar to Stonehenge, England.

▲ Thule was associated by the ancient Greeks with the aurora borealis, also called the Northern Lights.

THULE

Another mysterious Arctic realm is Thule, supposedly visited by the ancient Greek explorer Pytheas in the fourth century BCE. Pytheas

▲ The great temple of Hyperborea supposedly resembled Stonehenge, the prehistoric monument near Salisbury, England.

recorded that Thule was a six-day sail north of Britain and was near the "frozen sea." Later, classical writers placed Thule to the northwest of Britain and Ireland, beyond the Faroes, which means that Thule could only have been Iceland. But if so, who were the inhabitants that Pytheas claimed to have found there? Pytheas described them as farming people, producing grain, fruit, dairy products, and honey. Yet, according to conventional history, Iceland was not settled until the Vikings arrived there in the ninth century CE.

FACT HUNTER

STONEHENGE

- **WHAT IS IT?**
It's a prehistoric monument in southern England, composed of earthworks surrounding a circular setting of large standing stones.

- **WHEN WAS IT BUILT?**
Most archaeologists believe that the stones were erected between 3000 BCE and 2200 BCE.

- **WHAT WAS IT USED FOR?**
The culture that built it left no written records. However, scholars have speculated that it was used as an astronomical hub or as a religious site for sun worshippers, possibly the Hyperboreans.

SHAMBHALA

Shambhala is a mythical kingdom in the Tibetan Buddhist tradition. It is often associated with Shangri-La, but the latter is a fictional place, invented by British author James Hilton in his 1933 novel *Lost Horizon*. *Shambhala* is a Sanskrit term meaning "place of peaceful happiness." It came to be regarded as a perfect place hidden in a Himalayan valley.

NOT A PHYSICAL PLACE?

Shambhala has been located at various sacred sites in or near Tibet, including the capital, Lhasa, and Potala, the former residence of the Tibetan spiritual leader, the Dalai Lama. However, His Holiness the 14th Dalai Lama said that Shambhala is not a physical place, but somewhere that can be arrived at only through spiritual enlightenment.

HUNZA

This has not prevented people from seeking Shambhala. In the 1920s, two Russian expeditions tried and failed to find it. Some believed it to be Hunza, a thousand-year-old principality in northern Pakistan. This remote and verdant valley was said to have been populated by a mainly

◀ Shambhala, if it exists, is a place of great beauty and tranquility.

▲ Shangri-La, in China's Yunan Province, is a tourist destination named after the fictional paradise of James Hilton's novel.

Buddhist community, which spread its influence to nearby Kashmir.

AGARTHA

Others have linked Shambhala to Agartha, another mythical kingdom located underground. Agartha is apparently lit by its own subterranean sun and populated by people 4 m (13 ft) tall, who will one day fulfil an ancient prophecy by establishing their divine leader as king of the world.

FACT HUNTER

SHANGRI-LA

- **WHAT IS IT?**
In James Hilton's novel, Shangri-La was a mystical, harmonious valley located in the Kunlun Mountains.

- **WHAT IS ITS SIGNIFICANCE?**
Shangri-La has come to be used as a term for any earthly paradise or permanently happy land, isolated and insulated from the outside world.

- **WHAT IS ITS CONNECTION TO SHAMBHALA?**
Hilton was inspired by stories of Shambhala, which was being sought by Eastern and Western explorers at the time he wrote his novel. Shangri-La literally means "Shang [a region of Tibet] Mountain Pass."

BIGFOOT: FIRST IMPRESSIONS

The native peoples of North America are the source of the oldest stories about Bigfoot, or Sasquatch. Different tribes have different names for it. They called it *chenoo* or *kiwakwe*. They all describe a creature covered in fur that looks like a large human and lives in remote forested areas.

WILD MAN OF THE WOODS

As early as 1793, European settlers in North America were reporting sightings of a "hairy ape man." A legend soon grew up of a "wild man of the woods." This was seemingly supported by several newspaper reports of scary encounters where hunters and trappers in the area stumbled across apemen in the woods during the nineteenth and early twentieth centuries.

▼ Apemen have been sighted in lots of different countries and have been given many different names. Could they in fact belong to the same species?

Yowie • Orange Pendak • Yeren • Yeti • Maricoxi • Wildman

◀ Could the forests around Mount St. Helens be home to the Sasquatch?

STOLEN AWAY

That same summer, a Canadian, Albert Ostman, claimed he was seized by Sasquatches. He was camping in the mountains of British Columbia when one night he was carried away in his sleeping bag by four hairy, apelike people. They held him captive for several days.

BATTLE OF APE CANYON

In July 1924, an Oregon newspaper ran a story about a group of gold prospectors in the Mount St. Helens region who came under attack from a group of Sasquatches. According to their account, they first saw a creature while they were getting water. It was over 2 m (6.5 ft) tall and was watching them from behind a tree.

That night, three Sasquatches attacked the men's cabin, pounding the walls with large rocks. Two creatures climbed on the roof. However, by the next morning, the creatures had gone.

Examining The Evidence

Cryptids

The creatures described in this chapter are all legendary creatures, or cryptids. Do they actually exist? It's certainly true that many people claim to have seen them. However, scientists argue that eyewitness reports are not enough evidence to prove a creature exists. Witnesses might mistake a sighting of one creature for something else, or be the victims of hoaxes.

MONSTERS 83

BIGFOOT: THE SIGHTINGS CONTINUE

Four years after Albert Ostman's encounter, another man claimed to have been carried away in the night. Muchalat Harry was a fur trapper from Vancouver Island, British Columbia, who said he was taken from his camp and captured by around 20 Sasquatches. Seeing a pile of bones nearby, he became terrified that he would be eaten, but he escaped to tell his tale.

RUBY CREEK INCIDENT

George and Jennie Chapman and their three children lived near the village of Ruby Creek, British Columbia. During the summer of 1941, while George was away working, Jennie and her eldest son claimed to have spotted a gigantic hairy man near their house. He cried out and began striding toward them. Alarmed, they fled.

▲ Bigfoot is often described as a giant hairy man.

Next, Jennie shepherded her children out of the house under a blanket, hoping the Sasquatch wouldn't see them.

◀ This photograph of "Bigfoot" was taken by a backpacker on November 17, 2005.

THE FAMILY VANISHED

When George arrived home two hours later, he found the door to the outhouse smashed in, food scattered around and half eaten, and giant footprints in the soil. It was with relief that he found his family safe at Jennie's father's house. On five more nights after that, the family heard the cry of the Sasquatch and found footprints not far from their house.

STRANGE STORIES

WILLIAM ROE'S ACCOUNT

Roe was a hunter and trapper living in Alberta, Canada. One day in October 1955, he was approaching an old, abandoned mine in Tête Jaune Cache when he saw what he took to be a grizzly bear in the bushes. When the creature emerged into the clearing, he saw it wasn't a bear. It looked more like a giant hairy man. It squatted down and began eating leaves off a bush. Then it caught his scent and looked at him. Standing up, it walked away rapidly. Roe raised his rifle to shoot, but then the creature glanced back and Roe said he saw a spark of humanity in its eyes. Suddenly, he felt that killing this creature would be murder, so he let it go.

BIGFOOT: HITTING THE HEADLINES

Modern interest in Bigfoot began in 1958, sparked by events at Bluff Creek in Northern California. On the morning of August 27, a construction crew building a road through this area turned up for work to discover some strange footprints in the soil. They were described as looking like naked human footprints. However, they were different in one crucial way—they were much bigger.

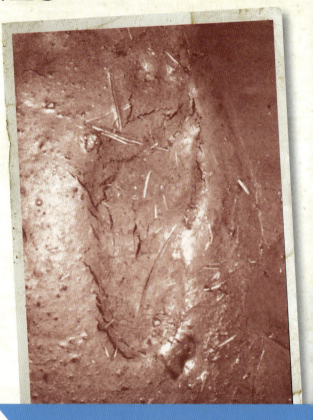

▲ Jerry Crew found enormous footprints in the soft mud at Bluff Creek.

FOOTPRINTS

The man who discovered the prints was bulldozer operator Jerry Crew. When more prints appeared on October 1, he made a plaster of paris cast of one of them and was photographed with it for the local newspaper. The story was taken up by newspapers across the United States and the world.

Several cryptozoologists (people who study cryptids) visited the site and made more footprint casts, as well as collecting eyewitness reports of encounters. Later, it emerged that the head of the construction firm, Ray Wallace, owned a pair of gigantic wooden feet. He had faked many of the Bigfoot prints. However, whether he faked them all is open to debate.

chased by a Sasquatch in the hills above Alpine, Oregon. In June 1963, Stan Mattson reported witnessing a female Sasquatch with a baby catching small fish near Yale, in Washington State. And in October 1966, the Corey family reported a visit by a Sasquatch that was 2 m (7 ft) tall. They said it killed the family dog.

▲ This photographer is measuring a Bluff Creek footprint before taking a picture.

THE REPORTS MULTIPLY

After the Bluff Creek episode, stories of Bigfoot encounters came flooding in. In the summer of 1959, a woman named Mrs. Bellevue was startled by a humanlike ape watching her from behind some trees while she was camping in British Columbia. In 1961, Larry Martin claimed he was

Examining The Evidence

Did Wallace fake all the Bluff Creek footprints?

Some people believe that practical joker Wallace was responsible for all the footprints found at Bluff Creek, including the original ones found by Jerry Crew. They say that his company was falling behind with its work and Wallace wanted to come up with a reason to extend the deadline. On the other hand, Wallace was away from the state on business when at least some of the tracks appeared. Believers in the Sasquatch argue that Wallace took to his hoaxing after the first prints appeared in Bluff Creek, so that he could exploit them.

BIGFOOT: FILMING A SASQUATCH

On October 20, 1967, Roger Patterson filmed a mysterious creature in Bluff Creek, Northern California. This is the most important single piece of evidence for the existence of Bigfoot. Patterson and his companion, Bob Gimlin, have been called heroes by some but described by others as frauds or victims of a hoax.

▲ This famous image from the Patterson Film shows the Bigfoot glancing behind it.

PATTERSON'S STORY

Patterson and Gimlin were both part-time rodeo riders. They headed into the wilderness that October with a camera in search of Sasquatch. They had been riding for some hours, apparently, when they reached a creek running through a canyon. Beside the creek, about 8 m (25 ft) from them, they saw a creature. It also spotted them and began walking away. Patterson immediately grabbed the camera and ran after the Sasquatch.

He tripped and fell at one point but kept filming. The creature turned to look at him as it walked. Soon it passed around a bend and out of sight.

OTHER EVIDENCE

Since 1967, other Sasquatch footage has come to light. However, none matches the quality of the Patterson Film.

night in Northern California, shows a similar-looking creature moving in the beam of a car's headlights.

The Manitoba footage (2005), shot on the banks of the Nelson River, Manitoba, shows a strange figure on the opposite bank. It is too far away for people to be sure what it is, though.

▲ Freeman with his casts of "Bigfoot prints." He found so many that some of his colleagues became suspicious.

Examples include the Freeman footage, shot in 1994 by forestry worker Paul Freeman near Walla Walla, Washington State. It shows a hairy, humanlike figure crossing a path and then disappearing into the woods. The Redwoods footage (1995), filmed on a rainy

Examining The Evidence

What does the Patterson Film show?

Bigfoot researchers who have studied the footage suggest it is a female Bigfoot, as two mammary glands are visible on its front. Some people have questioned the authenticity of the footage and say that if it is played at a slightly faster speed, it looks like a human in a costume. However, some things do make scientific sense.

For example, biologists have said that for such a creature to walk upright, it would need an extended heel—which the creature in the film has. Movie industry experts have said the footage was not made using special effects.

THE SKUNK APE

In the mid-1960s, Florida police received several reports claiming that an apelike creature was living in the state's swampland. It sounded similar to Bigfoot, except for one thing—it smelled like a mixture of rotten eggs and manure. One witness said it had the scent of a skunk rolling around in refuse. It soon became known as the Skunk Ape.

▶ This photograph allegedly shows a Florida Skunk Ape.

▲ An artist's impression of Jennifer Ward's encounter with a Skunk Ape.

moving through forests bordering the Anclote River in Florida. He said it had a rancid, putrid scent. Reports of the Skunk Ape continued to flow in, and in August 1971, Henry Ring, a Broward County rabies control officer, was sent out to investigate. He found no apes but did discover some strange, apelike tracks.

The sightings continued to be reported through the 1980s and 1990s. In 2000, a group of tourists in the Everglades saw a large, apelike animal moving around in a swamp. Later, it was seen crossing the road outside the house of a local fire chief. One man took a photograph of the beast as it retreated into swampland.

FOUL SCENT

In 1966, Eula Lewis of Brooksville, Florida, reported being chased into her house by an apelike creature with a round head and long arms. In July of the same year, Ralph Chambers spotted what he called a "hairy man"

STRANGE STORIES

CREATURE IN THE CELLAR

In August 1979, a team of workmen was sent to demolish a remote farmstead near Ochopee, Florida. They noticed a foul smell coming from the cellar and assumed an animal had died in there. Two hours later, one of the men saw a creature climb out of the cellar. The man yelled and the other men came running. They saw the creature walk upright across open ground before disappearing into some trees. It was about 5 ft (1.5 m) tall and covered in reddish hair.

THE YETI

In 1921, a team of British mountaineers scaling the north face of Mount Everest noticed dark shapes moving in the snow above them. When they reached the site, they found large, humanlike footprints. Their Sherpa guides called the creature *metoh-kangmi*, which translates as "abominable snowman." The other name for it is the yeti.

▲ The photograph that sparked international interest in the yeti.

FOOTPRINTS IN THE SNOW

Four years later, N.A. Tombazi, a Greek photographer, was on an expedition in the Himalayas when he and his guides caught sight of a humanlike figure in the distance. The creature soon departed but again left strange footprints in the snow. Footprints that may have belonged to a yeti were also found on Everest by mountaineers Eric Shipton and Michael Ward in 1951. They were seen again by Sir Edmund Hillary and Sherpa Tenzing Norgay on their famous climb to the summit of that mountain in 1953.

A TAILLESS ANIMAL

Over the years, further encounters have been reported. In 1974, a Sherpa girl and her yaks were apparently attacked by a yeti. In 1976, a report told of how six forestry workers came across a strange, tailless animal covered

▶ Could the yeti be an ape that has adapted to cold climates?

in reddish-brown fur. Some hair samples were obtained to back up these reports. The hairs were studied but could not be identified.

In 1986, British physicist Tony Woodbridge—who was doing a sponsored solo run in the Himalayas—spotted what he believed to be a large, hairy, powerfully built creature about 150 m (500 ft) away. However, closer examination of the photographs he took convinced Woodbridge it had been a tree stump.

EYEWITNESS TO MYSTERY

HAIRY MAN

Pang Gensheng, a farmer in Shaanxi in China, describes an encounter with a yeti: "In the summer of 1977 I went to Dadi Valley to cut logs. Between 11 a.m. and noon I ran into the 'hairy man' in the woods. It came closer and I got scared, so I retreated until my back was against a stone cliff … I raised my ax, ready to fight for my life. We stood like that, neither of us moving for a long time. Then I groped for a stone and threw it at him. It hit his chest. He uttered several howls and rubbed the spot … Then he turned … and leaned against a tree, then walked away …"

THE BIG GRAY MAN

It is said that on the mountain of Ben MacDui, in the Scottish Highlands, there lurks a huge and terrifying creature. Locals call it Am Fear Liath Mor, or the Big Gray Man. Some see it as an old figure in robes, a giant, or even a devil. The creature, so they say, is physically threatening and causes terrifying panic in those who come near it. Scientists have suggested that the creature may be a result of hallucinations caused by isolation or exhaustion.

▲ Some believe that strange creatures roam the slopes of Ben MacDui.

▲ Is the Big Gray Man a living creature? Or could it possibly be a supernatural apparition? Nobody knows for sure.

FOREST CHASE

In the early 1990s, three men were walking in a forest close to the mountain when they spotted a humanlike figure running across the track. A few weeks later, the men were driving in the area when they realized they were being followed by the same being. It kept pace with the car, even at speeds of 72 km/h (45 mph), before eventually disappearing.

FOOTSTEPS

In 1891, Norman Collie, an experienced climber, was descending through mist from the peak of Ben MacDui when he heard footsteps behind him. At first, he assumed it was an echo of his own footfalls. But the noises did not match his movements. It sounded like a giant was following him. Terrified, he ran blindly for around 8 km (5 mi) down the mountain until he could no longer hear the noise.

FACT HUNTER

BROCKEN SPECTERS

- **WHAT ARE THEY?**
Optical illusions that can be seen on misty mountainsides or cloud banks when the Sun is low. The observer's shadow is cast onto low-lying clouds opposite the Sun.

- **WHAT VISUAL EFFECT DO THEY CAUSE?**
They create the illusion of a large, shadowy, humanoid figure.

- **WHY DOES THE FIGURE APPEAR SO LARGE?**
The magnification of size is an optical illusion that happens when the observer thinks their shadow is at the same distance as faraway land objects seen through gaps in the clouds.

THE LOCH NESS MONSTER

Of all the world's mythical beasts, perhaps the most famous is Nessie, the Loch Ness monster. Loch Ness is a freshwater lake in the Scottish Highlands, 38 km (24 mi) long and up to 300 m (1,000 ft) deep. Although stories of a creature in the loch have been told ever since 565 CE when Saint Columba was said to have seen one, it wasn't until the twentieth century that the phenomenon really took off.

EARLY SIGHTINGS

In April 1933, a local couple spotted an enormous animal rolling and playing in the water. Soon afterward, a fisherman saw it, describing it as having a long neck, a serpentine head, and a huge hump. He believed it to be around 9 m (30 ft) in length. In July of that year, a family from London almost crashed into a massive, dark, long-necked animal that strolled across their path and then disappeared into the water.

◀ Urquhart Castle overlooks Loch Ness.

▲ The famous "surgeon's photograph" of Nessie.

In June 1993, a couple was on the bank of the loch when they saw a huge creature in the water. They estimated it to be over 12 m (40 ft) long, with a giraffe-like neck.

FAMOUS PHOTO

Over the years, there have been many attempts to capture Nessie on film. One of the most famous photographs, showing the monster's head and neck, was published in 1934. The "surgeon's photograph," as it became known, was later revealed to be a fake.

SEARCHING FOR NESSIE

There have been about 3,000 similar sightings. The Academy of Applied Science in Boston, Massachusetts, launched the first scientific expedition in the early 1970s. Underwater cameras captured images of what looked like a flipper that was 2.4 m (8 ft) long and an unusual body that was 6 m (20 ft) long. However, a later expedition revealed the image to be of a tree stump.

EYEWITNESS TO MYSTERY

NECK LIKE A CONGER EEL

In early May 2001, at around 6 a.m., James Gray and Peter Levings were fishing on Loch Ness when Gray spotted a movement 140 m (460 ft) away and saw something sticking out of the water. Then the object began to rise: "Soon, it was about 1.8 m [6 ft] out of the water but seconds later it had become a black kind of blob as it disappeared. It had curled forward and gone down ... This was certainly no seal. It had a long black neck almost like a conger eel, but I couldn't see a head. It didn't seem to bend very much but as it went under it sort of arched and disappeared."

NESSIE: THE HUNT CONTINUES

The search for the Loch Ness monster continues to this day. In 1987, scientists carried out Operation Deepscan, an organized, structured sonar sweep of the loch. Deepscan didn't find the monster, but it did report various hard-to-explain sonar echoes moving around in the extreme depths of the loch.

STRANGE NOISES

In March 2000, a team of Norwegian scientists picked up bizarre grunting and snorting noises in the loch's water. They sounded very similar to noises recorded in a Norwegian lake that also has a monster legend attached to it.

▶ Could the Loch Ness monster be a survivor from the age of the dinosaurs? This digital image shows a plesiosaur called *Elasmosaurus*.

NESSIE'S LAIR

Relatively recent sonar explorations have revealed huge underwater caverns near the bottom of Loch Ness. These have been nicknamed Nessie's Lair. Some scientists suggest they may be big enough to hide a family of creatures. If the monster does exist, a breeding colony would be needed for its survival.

COULD NESSIE BE A PLESIOSAUR?

Experts have suggested that Nessie seems to bear a strong resemblance to a creature now thought to be extinct—the plesiosaur, a marine reptile not found on Earth for over 60 million years. Plesiosaurs had large flippers, a small head, and a large body. Sometimes they are described as "snakes threaded through the bodies of turtles."

Some cryptozoologists believe that a few of these animals may have been stranded in the loch after the Ice Age. But as a marine reptile, the plesiosaur's natural habitat was saltwater. It is very unlikely that it would be able to survive and adapt to the freshwater conditions of the lake. Meanwhile, the sightings continue, and the loch is now under 24/7 CCTV observation.

FACT HUNTER

LAKE MONSTER

- **WHAT IS IT?**
A lake monster is a freshwater-dwelling, large animal that is the subject of mythology, speculation, or local folklore but whose existence lacks scientific support. Nessie is one of the most famous lake monsters.

- **DO THEY REALLY EXIST?**
Most scientists believe lake monsters to be exaggerations of misinterpretations of known and natural phenomena or else fabrications and hoaxes. They may be seals, otters, deer, diving water birds, large fish, logs, mirages, or unusual wave patterns.

- **WHAT OTHER LAKE MONSTERS ARE THERE?**
Examples include the Thetis Lake monster (Thetis Lake, British Columbia, Canada), Bessie (Lake Erie, Ohio, United States), Auli (Lake Chad, Chad), and Brosno Dragon (Brosno Lake, Russia).

THE LUSCA

Around the Bahamas and the southeastern coast of the United States there are tales of a giant octopus that captures unwary swimmers and small boats. The people of the islands call it the Lusca and believe it lives in deep underwater caves.

MYSTERIOUS CARCASS

One evening in November 1896, two men were cycling along the coast just outside the town of St. Augustine, Florida, when they spotted a huge, silvery-pink carcass on the beach. It was 7 m (23) long, 5.5 m (18 ft) wide, and seemed to have multiple legs. It weighed 6–7 tonnes (7–8 tons).

The men informed Dr. Dewitt Webb, a local scientist, who came to examine the corpse. Webb was convinced it was some kind of enormous octopus.

▼ This nineteenth-century print shows a giant octopus attacking a galleon.

100 MONSTERS

However, other experts disagreed, saying it was probably just the head of a sperm whale. Further tests on samples from the corpse, carried out in 1971 and 1986, seemed to confirm that it was indeed part of a gigantic octopus. But even more detailed tests in 1995 suggested the carcass was actually part of a whale.

GIANT OCTOPUS

Locals say the Lusca can grow to over 23 m (75 ft) long and some say up to 60 m (200 ft). No octopus approaching that size has ever been found. However, on January 18, 2011, the body of what appeared to be a giant octopus washed ashore on Grand Bahama Island, in the Bahamas. According to eyewitness reports, the remains represented only a portion of the head and mouthparts of the original creature. Local fishermen estimated the total length of the creature to have been 6–9 m (20–30 ft).

RECORD BREAKER

Scientists suggest that the Lusca may, in fact, be a giant squid, which has been known to grow to very large sizes. The largest squid on record was a female giant squid that washed ashore on a New Zealand beach in 1887. It was 18 m (59 ft) long and weighed 1 tonne (1 ton).

STRANGE STORIES

THE CHICKCHARNEY

The Lusca is not the only cryptid that haunts the Bahamas. The Chickcharney is a creature resembling an owl that reportedly lives in the forests of Andros Island. According to legend, it is about 1 m (3 ft) tall, furry, feathered, and ugly. People who meet the Chickcharney and treat it well are rewarded with good luck. Those who don't will be the victim of hard times.

THE MONGOLIAN DEATH WORM

Under the burning sand dunes of the Gobi Desert there is said to lurk a creature so feared by the Mongolian people, they are scared even to speak its name. When they do, they call it the *allghoi khorkhoi*, or "large intestine worm," because this red, snakelike monster looks similar to a cow's intestines. In the West, the monster has come to be known as the Mongolian death worm.

DEATH FROM A DISTANCE

According to tales, this worm, measuring up to 1.5 m (5 ft) in length, can kill instantly. Some believe it spits a lethal toxin. Others say it emits an electrical charge. However it kills, it does so quickly and can do it from a distance.

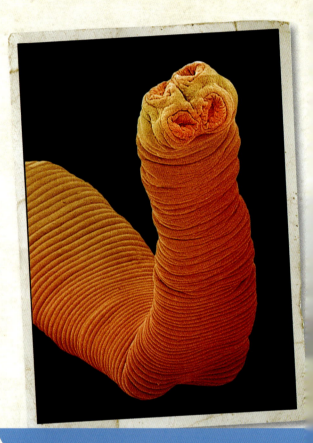

▲ This magnified image shows a parasitic tapeworm, which lives in the human gut. Could the Mongolian death worm be related to this real-life worm?

Mongolian nomads believe the giant worm covers its prey with an acidic substance that turns everything it touches yellow and corroded. Legend says that as the creature begins to attack, it raises half its body out of the sand and starts to inflate until it explodes, releasing the lethal poison over the unfortunate victim. The poison is so powerful, the prey dies instantly.

▲ The death worm is described as looking similar to a swollen intestine.

WHAT IS IT?

In recent years, Western investigators have searched for evidence of the creature's existence. One man, Ivan Mackerle, carried out many interviews and came to the conclusion that the death worm was more than just a legend. However, no one can say for sure what it is. Experts are certain it is not a real worm because the Gobi Desert is too hot an area for annelids to survive. Some suggest it may be a skink. However, skinks have little legs and scaly skin, while eyewitnesses insist the worm is limbless and smooth-bodied. The most probable explanation is that the death worm is a type of venomous snake.

STRANGE STORIES

THE MINHOCÃO

Another legendary wormlike creature is the Minhocão of southern Brazil. This giant creature allegedly lives at the fords of rivers, where witnesses have claimed to see it drag livestock under the water. According to an account written in 1877, the Minhocão can dig trenches big enough to divert rivers or overturn trees. It is said to have scaly black skin "as thick as pine tree bark," a piglike snout, and two tentacle-like structures protruding from its head.

MOTHMAN

In early November 1966, various sightings of a huge, strange "bird" were reported around Point Pleasant, West Virginia. On November 12, five gravediggers preparing a plot claimed they saw a "brown human being" take to the air from some nearby trees and pass over their heads. The creature came to be known as Mothman.

FLYING MONSTER

On November 15, two young couples were driving together in an area just outside Point Pleasant. As they passed an old generator plant, they noticed that its door appeared to have been ripped off. They then claimed to have seen two red eyes shining out of the gloom. The eyes belonged to a creature shaped like a man but more than 2 m (7 ft) tall, with wings

▲ According to witnesses, the Mothman had glowing red eyes.

folded against its back. As the creature approached, the young people ran away. Glancing behind, they saw it take to the air, rising straight up without flapping its wings. It had a 3 m (10 ft) wingspan and kept pace with their car despite the vehicle reaching high speed. The creature disappeared before they reached Point Pleasant.

BRIDGE DISASTER

In the year that followed, Mothman was seen by many witnesses, including firemen and pilots. Then, on December 15, 1967, the Silver Bridge linking Point Pleasant to Ohio suddenly collapsed, causing the death of 46 people. Mothman was rarely seen after that. Some people believe the bridge disaster may have been the monster's terrible final act.

EYEWITNESS TO MYSTERY

TERRIBLE, GLOWING EYES

On November 16, 1966, a young mother reported a scary incident. She said she was driving to a friend's house just outside Point Pleasant when she saw a strange red light in the sky. Arriving at her destination, she heard something rustling near her car. She recalled, "It rose up slowly from the ground. A big gray thing. Bigger than a man, with terrible, glowing eyes." As she fled into the house with her small daughter, the creature followed and stared in through the windows. The police were called, but by the time they arrived, the creature had disappeared.

THE OGOPOGO

Okanagan Lake is in British Columbia, Canada. It is around 160 km (100 mi) long and up to 300 m (984 ft) deep. The native Salish peoples believed in a terrible serpent, which they called *N'ha-a-itk*, or the "Lake Demon." They said the beast had a cave dwelling near the middle of the lake, and they would make sacrifices to please the monster.

THE MODERN LEGEND

European settlers initially scoffed at the legends. However, over the years the Ogopogo, as it came to be known, has established itself in the minds of many who live nearby. European immigrants started seeing strange phenomena in the lake during the mid-1800s. One of the first stories told of a man crossing the lake with his two tethered horses swimming behind. Some strange force pulled the animals under, and the man saved himself by cutting the horses loose.

▶ Could a monster lurk in the serene waters of Okanagan Lake?

▲ The Ogopogo seems like a more aggressive cousin of the Loch Ness monster.

MOVIE MONSTER

The Ogopogo was allegedly filmed in 1968. The footage shows a dark object propelling itself through shallow water near the shore. More footage, in 1989, showed a snakelike animal flicking its tail. Between August 2000 and September 2001, three local companies offered a $2 million reward to anyone who could find proof that the Ogopogo existed.

SIGHTINGS

Most alleged sightings have occurred around the city of Kelowna, near the middle of the lake. Witnesses say the creature is up to 15 m (50 ft) long, with green skin, humps, and a huge, horselike head.

A major sighting occurred in 1926 when the occupants of no fewer than 30 cars at Okanagan Mission Beach supposedly all saw the monster at the same time.

Examining The Evidence

What could it be?

British cryptozoologist Karl Shuker has categorized the Ogopogo as a "many hump" variety of lake monster. He has suggested it could be a kind of primitive serpentine whale such as *Basilosaurus*. However, others suggest the sightings are misidentifications of common animals such as otters, beavers, or lake sturgeon, or inanimate objects such as floating logs.

CROP CIRCLES

The beautiful geometric shapes known as crop circles have been appearing in fields for over 300 years. More than 5,000 have appeared in over 40 countries. Many are undoubtedly hoaxes. However, could some be real instances of mysterious forces at work?

UFOS AND EARTH FORCES

Some witnesses claim to have seen crop circles being made. They say an invisible line snakes at high speed through a field, pushing the stalks of crops aside. When it reaches a certain point, it begins to spin around, pushing the crops down, like the hands on a clock. When it has turned the full 360 degrees, the force vanishes, leaving the crops perfectly matted on the field floor. Tales of UFOs being spotted above fields the night before new formations appear are also common.

▲ Could crop circles be symbolic messages from an alien civilization?

Many people say crop circles are caused by freak weather conditions, such as tiny whirlwinds, rather than at the hand of aliens or strange forces. Others say they occur around historic areas of "high natural energy." They point to the fact that crop circles often appear near the sites of ancient forts, burial mounds, and standing stones, suggesting some sort of connection with humankind's prehistoric culture.

▲ Crop circles are not always circles. In fact, their shapes and patterns vary enormously.

STRANGE EFFECTS?

Video and audio recording devices have reportedly malfunctioned inside crop circles. Farmers have claimed that harvesting equipment fails to work near them. Some people have said they feel improved physical well-being in certain circles, while others have reported feelings of nausea, migraines, and fatigue. Some have seen animals behaving strangely, including horses and cats becoming nervous near patterns and flocks of birds veering around them.

STRANGE STORIES

THE MOWING DEVIL

The Mowing Devil is the title of an English pamphlet published in 1678, which is regarded by some as providing one of the first recorded examples of a crop circle. The pamphlet tells of a farmer who was outraged by the price a worker asked for mowing his field of oats. The farmer exclaimed that he would sooner the Devil mow it. That night, the field burst into flames, and the morning after, it was neatly mowed. The pamphlet's illustration shows a crop circle.

THE BERMUDA TRIANGLE

The Bermuda Triangle, or Devil's Triangle, is an area of ocean found off the southeastern tip of the United States. A widespread belief is that countless boats and planes have been inexplicably lost there. It is true that some high-profile disappearances have occurred in the region.

MYSTERY OF FLIGHT 19

The most famous loss in the triangle occurred on December 5, 1945. A squadron of five U.S. Navy Avenger torpedo bombers, known as Flight 19, set off from Florida for the island of Bimini. About an hour and a half into the flight, radio operators received a signal from the commander, Lt. Charles Taylor, saying his compasses weren't working, but he believed he was over the Florida Keys. In fact, he was over the Bahamas, and the

▼ According to popular belief, the Bermuda Triangle has been the site of countless unexplained disappearances over the years.

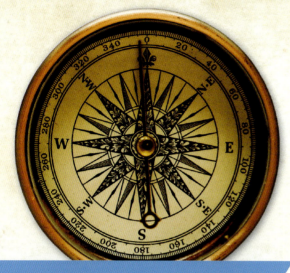

▲ One explanation is that magnets do not work normally in the Bermuda Triangle. This causes ships to lose their way.

THEORIES

All sorts of theories have been put forward to explain the loss of Flight 19 and other high-profile losses in the area. Some say that visiting UFOs enter an underwater base near Bermuda, or that evil marine creatures are responsible, or that the triangle is the site of a gateway to another dimension. Some blame huge clouds of methane gas escaping from the seabed.

directions he was then given took him farther away from land. After that, radio contact was lost and search craft were dispatched. One of the rescue craft lost communication and another exploded soon after take-off. Flight 19 has never been found.

NATURAL EXPLANATIONS

The U.S. Coast Guard believes that the losses in the area are caused by bad weather and human error. They say the Bermuda Triangle is no more treacherous than any other waterway.

STRANGE STORIES

THE DRAGON'S TRIANGLE

An area with a similar reputation to the Bermuda Triangle is the Dragon's Triangle, off the west coast of Japan. Japanese sailors call it *Ma no Umi*, which means "Sea of the Devil." Some say they've seen red lights and heard terrible noises. There is a legend that a sea monster, Li-Lung, lives there. In 1952, following numerous losses in the 1940s, the Japanese government dispatched a research vessel, the *Kaio Maru No.5*, to study the area. It disappeared without a trace.

THE NAZCA LINES

On the arid plateau of the Nazca Desert, in Peru, are some enormous and mysterious markings. Many are in the shape of people, animals, and plants. There are also hundreds of crisscrossing, randomly spaced lines, some forming squares, triangles, and other shapes. One line is over 14 km (8.7 mi) long.

▲ The Nazca Lines are only properly viewable from the air.

AERIAL VIEW

The lines appear to be centuries old, and locals have always known about them. Yet it was only in the 1930s, when regular air travel began in South America, that the truly remarkable nature of these lines was revealed. This is because the pictures and designs can only be appreciated from the air!

WHO CREATED THEM?

The pictures were produced using gravel, soil, and the under crust, which was an unusual shade. No one knows who created them because they cannot be dated with great enough accuracy. However, it is believed that they were created by the Nazca—a sophisticated people who were skilled in pottery, weaving, and architecture—who lived between about 100 BC and 800 CE.

WHAT WERE THEY USED FOR?

There are many theories that seek to explain the Nazca Lines.

▲ This aerial view appears to show a spider, one of the animal shapes found in the Nazca Lines.

the Nazca were early aviators who developed the world's first hot-air balloon. Another writer, Erich von Däniken, suggested the lines were runways for use by alien visitors to Earth.

Perhaps the most famous theory was put forward by Dr. Maria Reiche. She said that the lines were used as a sun calendar and an observatory for astronomical cycles. The animals, she theorized, were native representations of stellar constellations.

Depending on whom you believe, they are a calendar based on the stars and planets, they were used for religious ceremonies, or they showed underground sources of water. One theorist even suggests

EYEWITNESS TO MYSTERY

CLEANSING WIND

Dr. Maria Reiche explains how the lines have lasted for so long: "There are extremely strong winds here, even sandstorms, but the sand never deposits over the drawings. On the contrary, the wind has a cleansing effect, taking away all the loose material. This way, the drawings were preserved for thousands of years. It is also one of the driest places on earth, drier than the Sahara. It rains only half an hour every two years!"

THE PIRI REIS MAP

In 1929, a segment of an extraordinary map was unearthed in Istanbul, Turkey. The old gazelle-skin map seems to show part of the Atlantic Ocean and includes the Americas and Antarctica in striking detail.

ACCURATE MAPPING

The strange thing was that the map was created in 1513, only 21 years after Columbus landed in the Americas, and three centuries before Antarctica was discovered. It seems to show the coastline of Antarctica under the ice. The ice is up to 4 km (2.5 mi) thick, and the land under it wasn't mapped until 1949.

The map places the Falkland Islands at the correct latitude, despite the fact that they weren't discovered until 1592, and Greenland is shown as three separate islands, something that was only discovered in the twenty-first century.

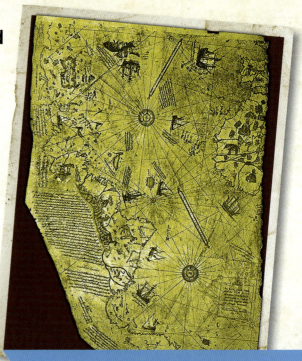

▲ The Piri Reis map appears to show the outline of Antarctica under the ice.

WHO CREATED IT?

The Piri Reis map is named after its creator, Muhiddin Piri, an admiral (*reis*) in the navy of Ottoman Turkey. On his travels he collected all kinds of charts of the coastlines and lands in the known world. He used these to compile his 1513 map of the world. The segment of the map that still exists is only a portion of the original.

▲ Is it possible that someone living in 1513 could have had an accurate knowledge of the Antarctic region?

MAP THEORIES

Some people believe that an ancient race of humans, using advanced but now lost technology, were able to record the details of Antarctica before it was covered with ice. Others suggest alien creatures mapped the planet, leaving their results behind to be copied by humankind.

Examining The Evidence

Antarctica—an inspired guess?

Experts point out that many maps from this time included imaginary continents in the South Atlantic, and Piri may just have been lucky with his guesswork. They say that ice has covered Antarctica for hundreds of thousands of years, at least. However, others claim that the continent may have been ice-free as late as 6,000 years ago.

KING ARTHUR

According to legend, Arthur was born sometime in the fifth century CE. Historians have uncovered several figures with claims to being the true Arthur. But was there ever such a person?

THE ROYAL CHILD

The legend says that Arthur was the illegitimate son of a British king, Uther Pendragon, and Igraine, wife of the Duke of Cornwall. The child was given away at birth, and raised completely unaware of his special lineage. When Uther died, the throne was empty. The magician Merlin set a sword, Excalibur, in rock, and stated that only the true king would be able to remove it.

THE ROUND TABLE

When young Arthur successfully pulled the sword from the stone, he was pronounced king. Eleven other British rulers rebelled against the young leader, but Arthur quashed their uprising and began a noble and glorious reign. Arthur married Guinevere and assembled a group of courageous and noble knights at his court in Camelot in the Vale of Avalon. They met at the fabled Round Table. The table's shape symbolized equality.

▲ The Sword in the Stone could only be released by the true king.

HISTORY AND LEGEND

The legend of Arthur and his knights of the Round Table may have grown out of an amalgamation (mixture) of the deeds of more than one person. In the sixth century, many Celtic realms had leaders named Arthur, and it's possible that they were all named in homage to a truly inspirational leader who ruled a generation before. We'll never know for certain, though.

▲ This engraving shows the great wizard, Merlin, finding Arthur abandoned as a young baby.

BETRAYED

One of Arthur's most trusted knights, Lancelot, had an affair with Guinevere and fled to Brittany. Arthur followed and waged war on his former friend, leaving his nephew, Mordred, as ruler in his absence. Mordred rebelled, and Arthur was forced to return home. Arthur fought and defeated Mordred, but he too was killed in the battle.

Examining The Evidence

Legendary leader

Historical evidence for an Arthurian-type figure can be found in a sixth-century work by Gildas, which refers to British soldiers being led by a man named Ambrosius Aurelianus.

The name Arthur appears in a ninth-century history written by a Welsh monk named Nennius. However, the legend of Arthur only really took hold in the twelfth century, when it featured in works by William of Malmesbury and Geoffrey of Monmouth.

GHOST SHIP

On November 7, 1872, the *Mary Celeste* left New York with a cargo of alcohol, bound for Italy. On board were the captain, his family, and a crew of seven. On December 4, the crew of another ship spotted the *Mary Celeste* sailing aimlessly ahead of them. The captain sent a boarding party to see what was going on. They found the *Mary Celeste* deserted but in perfectly sailable condition, with good supplies of food and water. Only the navigation equipment and the lifeboat were gone.

▼ A ship similar to the *Mary Celeste*.

▲ What ocean terror could have caused the entire crew to abandon ship?

Fearing the ship was about to explode, the captain ordered everyone into the lifeboat, planning to follow behind the *Mary Celeste* attached to a rope. But the rope must have snapped, and the *Mary Celeste* sailed off, leaving its crew stranded to perish in their small boat.

WHAT HAPPENED?

One version of events was that the crew had mutinied and then abandoned ship. This seems unlikely because it was a short journey, there were no signs of struggle on board, and the captain was viewed as a decent and respected man.

The most probable explanation was that the *Mary Celeste* hit a very bad storm. Alcohol spilled from the cargo barrels, and the ship's movement caused the galley stove to become unstable.

FACT HUNTER

GHOST SHIPS

- **WHAT ARE THEY?**
Ghost ships are ships found adrift with the entire crew either missing or dead.

- **HAVE THERE BEEN MANY GHOST SHIPS?**
Ghost ships were not uncommon during the nineteenth century. The Dutch schooner *Hermania* and the ship *Marathon* were both found abandoned but in perfect working order around the same time as the *Mary Celeste*.

- **SO WHY IS THE *MARY CELESTE* THE MOST FAMOUS GHOST SHIP?**
The *Mary Celeste* caught the public imagination, mainly thanks to the efforts of Sherlock Holmes' creator Arthur Conan Doyle, who wrote a story about it.

THE SECRET PRINCESS

In July 1918, the Russian Revolution claimed its most famous victims when the czar and his family were executed in Siberia. In 1920, a young woman in Berlin attempted suicide. She was rescued but could not identify herself, so was taken to an insane asylum. In 1922, she began claiming she was the Duchess Anastasia, the youngest daughter of the murdered czar.

ANNA OR ANASTASIA?

The woman, who now called herself Anna Anderson, declared that she had survived the assassination attempt, and one of the soldiers helped her get away. News of her claims soon spread, and she was visited by a number of relatives and acquaintances who had known the young princess.

▲ Here is Princess Anastasia before the assassination.

Anastasia's aunt, Princess Irene, declared her a fraud, but Irene's son Sigismund believed Anna was Anastasia, as did a family friend and the czar's doctor.

▲ Was this woman a survivor of the massacre of the royal family—or a Polish factory worker?

A FACTORY WORKER?

One theory suggests that Anna was a Polish woman named Franziska Schanzkowska, a former factory worker who had disappeared in Berlin only a day before Anna was rescued from the canal. Schanzkowska had received similar scars to Anna's from a factory accident. Anna was never able to prove her identity in a court of law. She died of pneumonia in 1984.

STRIKING SIMILARITIES

Anna was similar to the princess in many ways. She spoke excellent English, French, and German. She also had scars on her body that matched her description of her attempted execution. Experts declared that she looked very similar to Anastasia and their handwriting was identical. Anderson was also said to have an amazing knowledge of royal affairs.

Examining The Evidence

DNA tests

The debate over Anna Anderson did not end with her death. In 1991, the remains of the Russian royal family were discovered in Siberia. Scientists compared their DNA with samples of Anderson's hair and found no match. However, Anna did have extremely similar DNA results to blood samples taken from Franziska Schanzkowska's grand-nephew. Was the mystery solved? Not quite. When the Russian authorities uncovered the royal corpses, two were missing. One was the czar's son, Alexei. The other was his youngest daughter, Anastasia.

THE IMMORTAL COUNT

The Comte de Saint-Germain was first seen in Venice in 1710. According to witnesses, he looked to be between the ages of 40 and 50. However, people who met him decades later swore he hadn't aged a day. How can this be?

▲ Is it possible that the Comte de Saint-Germain had slowed his aging by supernatural means?

MAN OF TALENTS

Throughout his life, according to legend, Saint-Germain looked like a middle-aged man of average height. He had a deep understanding of art and music and created potions that he claimed were the elixir of youth. He was never seen to eat or drink, but he enjoyed socializing with the aristocracy.

SPY AND REVOLUTIONARY

The comte reached the height of his fame in Paris during the 1750s when he acted as a spy for King Louis XV. However, his friendship with the king earned him a number of enemies and he was forced to flee to England. He later resurfaced in Russia, where he apparently played a role in the 1762 revolution.

DEATH?

The story goes that by 1784, he had grown weary of life and died. But there is no official record of his death and no tombstone. Some say his death was staged. Certainly, further reports of Saint-Germain were reported. For example, the Countess of d'Adhémar said she met her old friend in 1789, 1815, and 1821, and each time he looked no older than her memory of him.

▲ If the legend of the comte is to be believed, he may have warned Marie Antoinette about the French Revolution.

He next appeared in Paris at the start of Louis XVI's reign, when he supposedly warned Queen Marie Antoinette of a possible revolution. When the king's minister ordered his imprisonment, he disappeared. He sought refuge at the castle of Count Charles of Hesse-Kassel in Schleswig-Holstein, Denmark.

Examining The Evidence

Who was he?

There were many theories about the real identity of the Comte de Saint-Germain, ranging from a Portuguese Jew to the son of the king of Spain's widow. According to a more recent study, he may have been the son of Prince Francis II Rákóczi of Transylvania. One of Prince Francis II Rákóczi's sons apparently died young, but may, in fact, have been raised by a family in San Germano, Italy, hence the comte's name, Saint-Germain.

AN UNCANNY CHILD

On May 26, 1828, a teenage boy stumbled up to the gates of Nuremberg, Germany. A local shoemaker approached him. The boy could barely speak but handed the man an envelope addressed to a captain in the Light Cavalry. Who was he?

▲ This is the house in which Kaspar Hauser was held prisoner.

STRANGE ABILITIES

The letter explained that the boy had been left with a poor worker who had kept him locked inside all his life, but the boy was now ready to serve in the king's army. The captain questioned the boy, but he had very few words. He could only write the words "Kaspar Hauser," and so this became his name.

Hauser acted like an infant child. He had no facial expressions, preferred to sleep sitting up, and was happiest in the dark. He also had powerful senses. He could apparently read in the dark, hear whispers from great distances, and identify people by their smell.

CAPTIVE LIFE

The captain placed the boy in the local prison, but the jailer took pity on him, and his children began to teach Hauser how to speak, write, and draw. By early 1829, Hauser had learned enough to write his autobiography.

▲ A portrait of Kaspar Hauser.

MYSTERIOUS DEATH

In October 1829, a stranger came to the house where Hauser was living and tried to murder him. Hauser was moved to the town of Ansbach, Germany. On December 14, 1831, Hauser went to the local park to meet a man who promised to reveal details about his mother. The man attacked Hauser. He died three days later aged 21.

Kaspar Hauser revealed that he had been kept in a tiny cell by a man whose face he never saw. He slept on a straw bed and lived on nothing but bread and water. One day, a man came to his cell and taught him to read a little and to write his name. The next day, Hauser and the man began a three-day journey that ended with his arrival in Nuremberg.

Examining The Evidence

Was Hauser a Baden prince?

After Hauser's death, a story began circulating that he was actually a prince, son of Karl of Baden and Stéphanie, Grand Duchess of Bavaria. The theory went that Karl's stepmother, the Duchess of Hochberg, switched him at birth with a sickly peasant child. The ill baby soon passed away. Karl himself died young, and on his deathbed claimed he had been poisoned. The throne then passed to his stepbrother, the Duchess of Hochberg's son. It is an unprovable theory.

INDEX

abduction 19
abominable snowman 92
Agartha 81
aircraft 6, 7, 8, 9, 11, 12, 13, 25, 28, 29, 62
Alcatraz 54–55
aliens 4, 5, 6, 10, 11, 14, 15, 16, 17, 19, 20, 22, 23, 24, 27, 31, 108, 113, 115
Anastasia, Duchess 120, 121
Andros Platform 72
animals 109, 112, 113
annelids 103
Antarctica 114, 115
apemen 82
apes 87, 90–91, 93
apparition 32–33, 38–39, 45, 95
Arnold, Kenneth 6, 8, 9
Arthur, King 116–117
assassination 120
asteroid 64, 65
Atlanteans 62, 63, 67, 68
Atlantic Ocean 57, 61, 63, 64, 65, 67, 68, 69, 70, 71, 73, 76
Atlantis 56–57, 60–73
automatic writing 37
aviators, ancient 62
Aztecs 67, 68

Bahamas 72, 73, 100, 101, 110
balls 6, 30
Basilosaurus 107
Basques 67
Bass Strait 28–29
bear 85
Ben MacDui 94, 95
Berlitz, Charles 61
Bermuda Triangle 110–111
Bertrand, Eugene 24, 25
Big Gray Man 94–95
Bigfoot 82–89, 90
Bimini Road 72, 73
Blavatsky, Helena 58–59
Bluff Creek, California 86, 87, 88
boats 68, 100, 110, 118, 119
Boleyn, Anne 45
Borley Rectory 52–53
Botta encounter, the 14–15
Brazil 19, 69, 77, 103
Brocken specters 95
burial 52, 108

Canada 85, 99, 106
castle 46, 96, 123
Chaffin, James 34
Chapman, George and Jennie 84–85
Chibcha Indians 69, 76
Chickcharney 101
child, uncanny 124–125
China 81, 93
cities of gold, 76–77
comet 64, 65
Conan Doyle, Arthur 37, 119
count, immortal 122–123
crash 10, 11, 13, 41, 43, 96
Crew, Jerry 86–87
crop circles 15, 108–109
cryptids 83, 86, 101
cryptozoologists 86, 99, 107
culture 32, 58, 59, 67, 68, 79, 108

death 13, 32, 33, 35, 41, 44, 45, 46, 47, 51, 55, 102, 103, 105, 121, 123, 125
Devil's Triangle 110
diver 74, 75
Donnelly, Ignatius 61
doppelgänger 38
Dragon's Triangle 111

Easter Island 59, 65
Edward, John 41
Egyptians 5, 62, 66, 67, 68
encounter 6, 14, 15, 16, 18, 22, 27, 28, 30, 31, 41, 73, 82, 84, 86, 87, 91, 92, 93
England 41, 43, 44, 52, 78, 79, 122
eruption 57, 65, 68
Everglades 91
evidence 7, 11, 17, 21, 25, 29, 31, 33, 42, 53, 57, 59, 60, 61, 66, 69, 71, 72, 73, 83, 87, 88, 89, 103, 107
execution 44, 45, 121
Exeter, New Hampshire 24–25
explorations 99
extraterrestrial life 31
eyewitness 6, 13, 17, 47, 49, 61, 63, 75, 83, 86, 93, 97, 101, 103, 105, 113

film 53, 88–89, 97, 107
Flight 19 110, 111
flying saucer 9, 10
foo fighters 6, 7
footprints 85, 86, 87, 92
footsteps 17, 53, 55, 95
forest 30, 56, 82, 83, 91, 95, 101
Fox family 48–49
Freeman footage 89

126

Friedman, Stanton 10, 11

ghost fliers 6
ghost hunter 53
ghost ship 118–119
ghost town 50
ghost(s) 5, 33, 34, 35, 36–37, 38, 39, 44, 45, 46–47, 50, 51, 52, 53, 55
giant 84, 85, 94, 95
Gimlin, Bob 88
Glamis Castle 46–47
Gobi Desert 102, 103
Godman Air Force Base 12
Gorique, Erkson 39
Greeks 78
Grey, Lady Jane 45

hallucination 19, 27, 33, 94
Hamilton, Tina 41
Hauser, Kaspar 124, 125
Hill, Betty and Barney 18, 19
Himalayas 92, 93
hoaxes 7, 83, 87, 88, 99, 108
Hopkins, Herbert 26, 27
Horseshoe Seamounts, the 70–71
humanoid 14, 15, 18, 95
Hunt, David 24

Hunza 80–81
Hynek, Josef 21
Hyperborea 78, 79
hypnosis 18–19

Incas 62, 77
India 58, 59
island 28, 54, 56, 57, 58, 59, 60, 62, 65, 67, 68, 69, 70, 71, 72, 73, 74, 75, 84, 100, 101, 110, 114

Japan 32, 65, 74, 75, 111

Kelly–Hopkinsville encounter, the 16–17
Kircher, Athanasius 60
Kuchisake-onna 32–33

lake monster 99, 107
legend 36, 46, 56, 57, 60, 61, 69, 76, 77, 82, 83, 98, 101, 102, 103, 106, 111, 116, 117, 122, 123
Lemuria 58–59, 64–65, 68, 69, 74–75, 76
Li-Lung 111
lights 6, 7, 8, 9, 14, 18, 24, 25, 27, 28, 29, 89, 111
lines 72, 108, 112, 113
Livingston 30–31

loch 96–99
Loch Ness monster 96–99, 107
Lusca 4, 100–101

Madagascar 58–59
Mandans 69
Manitoba footage 89
Mantell incident, the 12–13
map 19, 60, 71, 114–115
Marcel, Jesse 10
Mary Celeste 118, 119
mask 32, 77
Masse, Maurice 22, 23
Maya 68, 77
Mediterranean 56, 57
mediums 40
men in black 26–27
Merlin 116, 117
message(s) 12, 13, 34, 37, 39, 41, 53, 108
Mexico 58, 76
Minhocão 103
mirage 7, 99
Mongolian death worm 102–103
monster 5, 82–107, 111
Moors 76
Mothman 104–105
Mount Atlas 56, 60, 71
Mount Everest 92

Mount St. Helens 83
Mowing Devil, The 109
Mu 58, 59, 69
murder 35, 44, 49, 55, 85, 120, 125
Muscarello, Norman 24, 25
myth 60, 61, 65, 66, 69, 76, 77, 78, 80, 81, 96
mythology 99

Native Americans 54
Nazca Lines 112–113
Nessie 96–99
noises 23, 25, 30, 33, 48–49, 54, 95, 98, 111
North America 62, 63, 69, 82
nun 52

ocean floor 70, 71
octopus 100, 101
Ogopogo 106–107
Okanagan Lake 106, 107
Okinawa 74–75
Olmecs 58, 68
Operation Deepscan 98
optical illusion 95
Ostman, Albert 83, 84
Ouija board 41
Owen, Wilfred 37

127

Pacific Ocean 58, 65
Patagonia 77
Patterson Film 88, 89
Peru 112
phantom 36, 39, 45, 50, 53, 55, 76
pilot 6, 7, 12, 13, 15, 28, 105
Piri Reis map 114–115
plate tectonics 59
Plato 56, 57, 60, 63, 65, 67, 70, 71
plesiosaur 98, 99
poison 102, 125
Pole, Margaret 45
police 17, 20, 24, 25, 31, 90, 105
Pollock family 43
poltergeist 53
Poseidon 57
possession 42–43
prehistoric 32, 61, 67, 73, 75, 79
priest 43, 47, 60
princess, secret 120–121
psychic 40, 41
psychologist 42
pyramid 4, 62, 63

queen 45, 46, 123

Ray, Wallace 86–87
Redwoods footage 89
reincarnations 43
Roe, William 85
Romans 67, 77

Roswell 10–11
Round Table 116
Ruby Creek, British Columbia 84
Rudbeck, Olaus 60–61
Russian Revolution 120

Sagee, Emilie 38–39
Saint-Germain, Comte de 122, 123
samurai 32
Santorini 57
Sasquatch 82–85, 87, 88–89
scientists 19, 33, 83, 94, 98, 9, 100, 101, 121
Sclater, Philip 58
Scott, Sir Walter 47
Scottish Highlands 94, 96
séance 40
serpent 106
shadow(s) 9, 33, 51, 95
Shambhala 80–81
Shangri-La 81
Shine, Betty 40
ship(s) 39, 76, 111, 118, 119
Skunk Ape 90–91
smell 90, 91, 124
Society of Psychical Research 35
Socorro, New Mexico 20–21, 23
soldier(s) 36, 37, 54, 117, 120
sound(s) 22, 23, 30 55, 90, 95, 98
South America 58, 69, 77, 112
spacecraft 24
Spain 67, 76
Speight, William 36
spiritualists 37
squid 101
Squyres, William 48–49
standing stones 79, 108
Stephens, David 26
Stonehenge 78–79
surgeon's photograph 97
Sutton, Elmer 16, 17
swampland 90, 91

Taylor, Bill 16, 17
Taylor, Robert 30, 31
the Americas 68–69, 76–77, 114
the North, lost worlds of 78–79
Thule, 78–79
Tombstone, Arizona 50–51
Tower of London 44–45
tracks 31, 87, 91
trance 42
tsunami 65

UFOlogist 6, 11, 18, 21, 27
UFOs 6–9, 10, 11, 12, 13, 15, 16, 18, 19, 21, 22, 23, 25, 26, 27, 29, 30–31, 108, 111
United States Air Force (USAF) 11, 13

Valensole, France 22–23
Valentich, Frederick 28, 29
Vancouver Island, British Columbia 84
Vennum, Lurancy 42
volcano 56, 57, 60, 64, 65, 70

weather balloon 7, 10, 11
witnesses 6, 7, 10, 11, 21, 22, 25, 26, 27, 33, 38, 45, 83, 87, 90, 103, 105, 107, 108, 122
World War I 4, 36, 37
World War II 6, 40
worm 102, 103

yeti 82, 92–93

Zamora, Lonnie 20, 21